SAVING OUR LIVING EARTH

UNDERSTANDING

GLOBAL WARMING

REBECCA L. JOHNSON

LERNER PUBLICATIONS COMPANY · MINNEAPOLIS

For Earth's young and steadfast guardians

Text copyright © 2009 by Rebecca L. Johnson

Lerner Publications Company
A division of Lerner Publishing Group, Inc.
241 First Avenue North
Minneapolis, MN 55401 U.S.A.

Website address: www.lernerbooks.com

Library of Congress Cataloging-in-Publication Data

Johnson, Rebecca L.
    Understanding global warming / by Rebecca L. Johnson.
        p.   cm. — (Saving our living earth)
    Includes bibliographical references and index.
    ISBN 978-0-8225-7561-0 (lib. bdg. : alk. paper)
    I. Global warming. I. Title.
  QC981.8.G56J6454 2009
    363.738'74—dc22   2007048358

Manufactured in the United States of America
2 3 4 5 6 7 — DP — 14 13 12 11 10 09

CONTENTS

INTRODUCTION

Somewhere off the coast of northern Alaska, a polar bear stands on a chunk of sea ice. It is barely bigger than he is. The bear sees a larger, thicker chunk on the horizon. He hesitates. It's a long swim away. But he's desperate for food. The bear lunges into the water and starts paddling.

Polar bears live in the Arctic. This region includes the Arctic Ocean and the cold, treeless land that surrounds it. Seals are polar bears' favorite food. The bears hunt seals from the sea ice that forms on the ocean's surface. The bears crouch at the edge of the ice. They grab seals that come up to the water's surface to breathe.

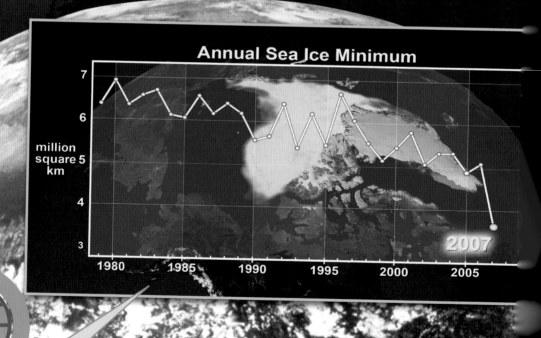

Above: The jagged line in the graph shows the overall decrease in Arctic sea ice since 1979. The background image shows sea ice (white) on the Arctic Ocean during summer 2007. The area covered by sea ice that year was the smallest on record. *Right:* A polar bear stands on a chunk of sea ice in the Arctic Ocean.

In winter, sea ice covers most of the Arctic Ocean. The ice stretches from northern Russia across the North Pole to Canada. When spring arrives, temperatures rise. The sea ice melts back, or retreats, from the land.

Until the late 1980s, the summer sea ice was always close enough to land that polar bears could easily reach it. That's no longer true. Arctic winters aren't as cold as they used to be. Summer temperatures are soaring, melting more and more ice. By midsummer, sea ice retreats as much as 200 miles (322 kilometers) from land.

Some polar bears drown as they try to swim to ice that is too far away. Others starve, unable to catch enough food. If the sea ice keeps shrinking, polar bears may not survive.

Why is this happening? Earth's average surface temperature is increasing. The Arctic is not the only place that's warming. Temperatures everywhere are rising. This worldwide change is called global warming.

Up until the early 2000s, many people doubted that global warming was anything to worry about. But research has erased that doubt. Global warming is changing Earth in ways that spell trouble for polar bears and other living things. It's changing in ways that affect people too. Global warming may be the greatest environmental challenge we've ever faced.

AT IS GLOBAL
RMING?

You've probably heard the phrase "global warming" hundreds of times. But what exactly does global warming mean?

Global warming isn't about having a hot day or week or month in one part of the world. It has to do with the average temperature worldwide. Simply put, global warming is the increasing of Earth's average surface temperature over time.

The current warming of Earth began in the mid-1800s. At first it was small and very gradual. But in the 1980s, Earth's average surface temperature began to rise more rapidly. It has been climbing ever since. Eleven of the twelve years from 1995 to 2007 were the hottest on record. Overall, Earth's temperature has risen 1.4°F (0.8°C) since about 1900.

UPS AND DOWNS VS. AVERAGES

Most graphs of recent global temperature show ups and downs. Some years are cooler, and others are hotter. Such differences from year to year are normal. What's more telling is to look at the graph as a whole. That way you see the average trend in temperature. And overall, the trend is up.

SOLAR ENERGY AND HEAT

Why is Earth warming? To answer that question, it's important to understand why Earth is warm in the first place. Think of the last time you were outside in the sun. That sunlight felt warm on your skin, right? Just like your skin, Earth's surface and everything on it is warmed by the sun.

Land, water, and most everything else on Earth absorbs energy from the sun. Earth's average surface temperature has increased rapidly since the 1980s.

The sun constantly radiates, or sends out, enormous amounts of energy. This solar energy travels through space toward Earth. Part of solar energy is visible light. Visible light is solar energy we can see. But we cannot see other parts of solar energy. For instance, infrared radiation (heat) is invisible to our eyes. So is ultraviolet light, which can cause sunburn.

Solar energy passes easily through Earth's atmosphere. Clouds reflect some solar energy back into space. So do snow and ice on the ground. But land, forests, water, and other things on Earth absorb incoming solar energy. And as Earth's surface absorbs solar energy, it warms. The warm surface, in turn, radiates heat.

THE ATMOSPHERE'S LAYERS

Earth's atmosphere is like a blanket of gases around the planet. It has several layers. Each layer blends into the one above it. The lowest layer, closest to Earth's surface, is the troposphere. This is where global warming is occurring. Some changes linked to global warming are also taking place in the stratosphere. That's the next layer up.

THE GREENHOUSE EFFECT

As heat radiates away from Earth's surface, some of it escapes into space. But not all of it. Certain gases in the atmosphere absorb some of the heat before it can escape. Then the gases reradiate that heat toward Earth. They absorb and reradiate heat over and over again. In effect, they trap a certain amount of heat in the atmosphere. Thanks to these heat-trapping gases, Earth's surface and the air just above it stay warm enough for living things to survive.

Scientists call this heat-trapping process the greenhouse effect. That's because Earth's atmosphere works somewhat like the clear covering of a greenhouse.

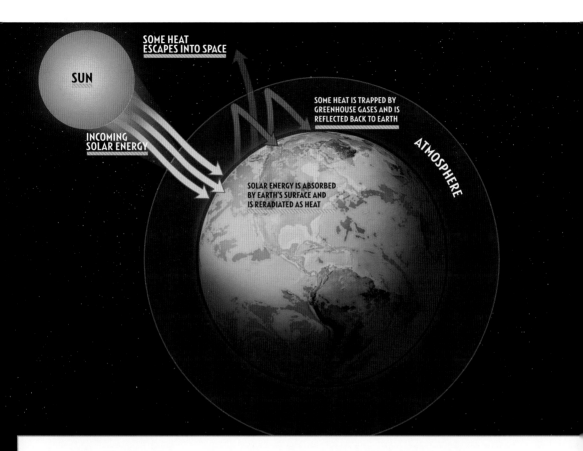

SUN

SOME HEAT
ESCAPES INTO SPACE

INCOMING
SOLAR ENERGY

SOME HEAT IS TRAPPED BY
GREENHOUSE GASES AND IS
REFLECTED BACK TO EARTH

SOLAR ENERGY IS ABSORBED
BY EARTH'S SURFACE AND
IS RERADIATED AS HEAT

ATMOSPHERE

Carbon dioxide and other greenhouse gases in the atmosphere trap some of the heat coming up from Earth's sun-warmed surface. This heat-trapping process is the greenhouse effect.

Sunlight passes through the greenhouse's roof and walls. Solar energy warms the things inside. Then those warm objects radiate heat. But the heat can't travel back out through the glass or plastic. It stays in the greenhouse, raising the temperature inside.

Earth's greenhouse effect is a lot more complicated than what happens inside a greenhouse. What makes Earth's greenhouse effect unique are the heat-trapping gases in the atmosphere. Scientists call them greenhouse gases. And they are the key to global warming.

WATER VAPOR AND CARBON DIOXIDE

What are the atmospheric gases that help keep Earth warm? The two most abundant greenhouse gases are water vapor and carbon dioxide.

Water vapor is water in its gas form. Water vapor gets into the air through evaporation. When water in rivers, lakes, and oceans is warmed by the sun, some is warmed enough to change to water vapor. The water vapor rises into the atmosphere.

Carbon dioxide is a colorless, odorless gas. It is made of one atom of carbon and two atoms of oxygen. Scientists know it as CO_2. Carbon dioxide is not just in the air. It's also in your body. Your cells produce carbon dioxide as a waste product. You get rid of it every time you breathe out. So do lots of other living things. Carbon dioxide is also produced when something burns. It's made when dead plant and animal matter decays (rots) too.

This forest fire is releasing carbon dioxide into the air.

Most living things produce and release carbon dioxide. But plants and algae (plantlike organisms that live in wet places) also take in carbon dioxide. They absorb it from air or water. They use it in a process called photosynthesis. Photosynthesis uses energy from sunlight to change carbon dioxide into food (sugar) for the plants or algae.

THE CARBON CYCLE

Carbon turns up in many kinds of molecules, not just carbon dioxide. In fact, carbon is just about everywhere in the natural world. For example, carbon is in the cells of all living things. The world's oceans contain carbon. Some of it is dissolved in the water. Huge amounts are stored in thick sediments (mud and sand) on the ocean floor. On land,

ATOMS AND MOLECULES

Everything in the world, including gases in the air, is made of molecules. A molecule is the smallest part of a substance that has all the traits of that substance. Molecules are made up of even smaller bits called atoms. A molecule of water includes two atoms of hydrogen (H) and one atom of oxygen (O). So scientists call water H_2O.

Stingrays glide along the ocean floor in the southern Atlantic Ocean. Carbon is stored in the mud and sand on the bottom of the ocean.

carbon is part of every plant leaf and stem. And since dead plants (and animals) often end up becoming part of the soil, soil has a lot of carbon too.

Chances are that the carbon atoms in any given molecule have been a lot of places. They have traveled far and wide over millions of years. That's because carbon moves among living things, the land, the atmosphere, and the oceans in the carbon cycle.

Some carbon moves quickly through the carbon cycle. Imagine lying on thick green grass. Grass blades just inches from your nose absorb carbon dioxide from

Carbon cycles through the natural world in many ways. One way is in molecules of carbon dioxide. Living things, decomposing material, and the burning of fuels all release carbon dioxide. Plants and algae take in carbon dioxide from air and water. The ocean absorbs some atmospheric carbon dioxide. It also releases carbon dioxide back into the air.

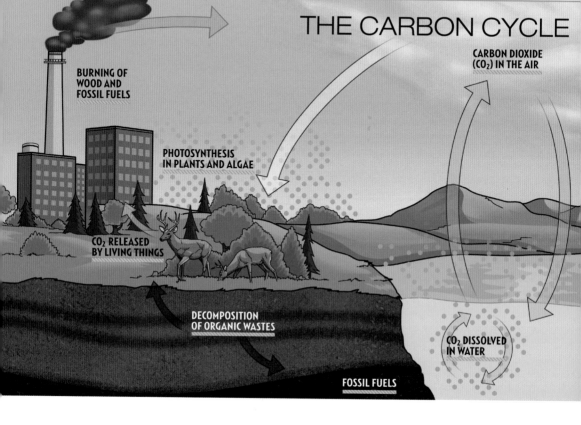

THE CARBON CYCLE

CARBON DIOXIDE (CO_2) IN THE AIR

BURNING OF WOOD AND FOSSIL FUELS

PHOTOSYNTHESIS IN PLANTS AND ALGAE

CO_2 RELEASED BY LIVING THINGS

DECOMPOSITION OF ORGANIC WASTES

CO_2 DISSOLVED IN WATER

FOSSIL FUELS

the air you breathe out. They use the carbon dioxide to make sugar. Some of the sugar gets stored in the grass blades. A week later, you mow the grass. The clippings fall to the ground. Within a few days, they begin to decay. Some of the carbon in the decaying clippings moves back into the air as carbon dioxide. It's ready to be taken up by grass again.

Some of the rest of the carbon becomes part of the soil. That soil carbon may stay put for a while. A year or more could pass before it moves to another part of the carbon cycle. Other carbon can stay in the ground for much longer. Deep underground in some parts of the world are rich deposits of carbon. This carbon came from plants that died millions of years ago. They were covered with soil or water before they had a chance to decay. Instead, pressure and heat in the ground gradually turned them into fossil fuels such as oil, coal, and natural gas. Fossil fuels contain enormous amounts of carbon. All that carbon has been stored since dinosaurs roamed Earth.

WARMING POWER

Just how powerful is an atmospheric greenhouse effect? Some of our nearest neighbors in space have helped scientists answer that question. Mars *(above)*, the fourth planet from the sun, has a very thin atmosphere. It has almost no heat-trapping power. Almost all the heat coming from Mars' sun-warmed surface escapes into space. The result? The average surface temperature of Mars is a numbing −58°F (−50°C). Compare that to Venus, the second planet from the sun. Venus's atmosphere contains far more heat-trapping gas than Earth's atmosphere. The average temperature on Venus is a searing 778°F (414°C). That's hot enough to melt lead!

13

OTHER GREENHOUSE GASES

Two other naturally occurring substances are also important greenhouse gases. One is methane, another colorless, odorless gas. Methane is made of carbon and hydrogen. Most methane in the atmosphere comes from natural processes. Cows burp up methane as they digest their food. Decaying things release methane into the air. So does farming certain kinds of crops, especially rice.

Nitrous oxide is a greenhouse gas made of nitrogen and oxygen. This gas is colorless but has a slightly sweet smell. Bacteria in soils and in the ocean produce nitrous oxide. Livestock wastes, nitrogen fertilizers, and some industrial processes are also sources of nitrous oxide.

Several human-made chemicals also act as powerful greenhouse gases. Two of these chemicals are chlorofluorocarbons (CFCs) and hydrofluorocarbons (HFCs).

Cows graze in a field. As cows digest food, they burp up methane gas. Their waste also is a source of nitrous oxide.

TOO MUCH OF A GOOD THING

Water vapor, carbon dioxide, methane, and nitrous oxide all trap heat radiating from Earth's surface. These greenhouse gases are like a furnace's thermostat. If you turn up the thermostat, the room gets warmer. Adding more greenhouse gases to the atmosphere increases the atmosphere's heat-trapping power. They create a

GREENHOUSE GAS AND OZONE DESTROYER

In the last century, CFCs were used in refrigerators, air conditioners, and aerosol cans. Then scientists showed that these chemicals were escaping into the air. They were destroying ozone molecules. Ozone molecules form a protective layer in the stratosphere. This ozone layer absorbs powerful ultraviolet rays coming from the sun. It prevents most of these dangerous rays from reaching Earth's surface. A thinner ozone layer lets in more of the harmful rays. CFCs also turned out to be powerful, heat-trapping greenhouse gases. Many countries banned CFCs in the 1990s. But CFCs already in the atmosphere will stay there for many years.

stronger greenhouse effect.

A stronger greenhouse effect is what global warming is all about. Scientists are convinced that most of Earth's recent warming is the result of too much of a good thing. It's happening largely because huge amounts of greenhouse gases are entering the atmosphere. All those heat-trapping molecules are turning up Earth's thermostat. They are raising the planet's average surface temperature.

Of all the greenhouse gases, carbon dioxide is the biggest culprit in global warming. People do many things that release carbon dioxide into the air. But by far the most significant is burning fossil fuels. These fuels provide power around the planet. When they burn, however, most of the carbon they contain moves into the air in heat-trapping molecules of carbon dioxide.

15

CHAPTER TWO

TURNING UP THE HEAT

You flip a switch, and the lights come on. You turn on the television. You heat something in the microwave or play a game on your computer. Think of how many times you use electricity every day!

Where does the electricity come from? Most of it comes from power plants. And most power plants burn coal to generate electricity. The more electricity people use, the more fossil fuels must be burned to generate electricity. The result is that more carbon dioxide is released into the atmosphere.

16

POWERING A WAY OF LIFE

Cars, buses, and trucks run on gasoline or diesel fuel. Both come from oil, another fossil fuel. Many houses, schools, malls, hospitals, and offices have heating systems that burn oil or natural gas. Natural gas is a fossil fuel too.

Farmers planted and harvested the grains in your breakfast cereal with machines that burn diesel fuel. Factories powered by coal or oil made the package for the cereal. Trucks burning gasoline or diesel fuel transported the packages to the grocery store. And the store's bright lights, coolers, freezers, and cash registers all run on electricity.

The more electricity people use, the more fossil fuels must be burned to generate electricity.

Left: Smoke billows into the air at this coal-burning power station in Yunnan, China, in 2007. Coal-burning power stations release a lot of CO_2 into the atmosphere. *Below:* The cars, trucks, and buses on this six-lane highway in New Jersey all burn fossil fuels.

The world runs on fossil fuels. Worldwide, people burn hundreds of millions of tons of coal, oil, and natural gas every year. These carbon-rich fuels make our modern way of life possible. But this way of life has serious consequences for the planet.

THE FOSSIL FUEL REVOLUTION

Coal, oil, and other fossil fuels didn't always play such a big role in life. People didn't start using them in large amounts until the Industrial Revolution began. Up until that time, most things were made by hand. But around 1800, machines took over many kinds of manufacturing tasks. Factories full of machines sprang up in Europe and the United States. The energy to run all those machines and factories came from burning fossil fuels, especially coal.

The internal combustion engine arrived on the scene in the late 1800s. Powered by gasoline, this engine was used in the first successful automobiles. Within a few decades, millions of cars and trucks were on the road.

Over the past two hundred years, people have added enormous amounts of carbon dioxide to the atmosphere by burning fossil fuels. In 2005 the burning of fossil fuels put 7.9 billion tons (7.17 billion metric tons) of carbon, in the form of carbon dioxide, into the atmosphere. Carbon emissions increase every year.

MAKING ELECTRICITY AROUND THE WORLD

As of 2007, 66 percent of the electricity generated worldwide came from burning coal, oil, and natural gas. In some parts of the world, fossil fuel use for generating electricity was far above this average. For example, 82 percent of the electricity produced in eastern and southern Asia came from fossil fuels. In the Middle East, it was a whopping 93 percent!

TOP TEN CO$_2$ EMITTERS

Country	Total 2004 CO$_2$ emissions (in millions of metric tons)	Percent increase since 1990	2004 CO$_2$ emissions per person (in metric tons)
United States	6,046	25	20.6
China*	5,007	109	3.8
Russia	1,524	−23	10.6
India	1,342	97	1.2
Japan	1,257	17	9.9
Germany	808	−18	9.8
Canada	639	54	20.0
United Kingdom	587	1	9.8
South Korea	465	93	9.7
Italy	450	15	7.8

Source: United Nations Development Programme

* CO$_2$ emissions from China do not include emissions for Taiwan, Province of China.

The data in this chart refer to the CO$_2$ emissions from the use of fossil fuels, gas flaring, and production of cement. For many years, the United States was the world's largest emitter of carbon dioxide. In 2007 researchers announced that China had surpassed the United States. China emits more carbon dioxide than any other country. Most of China's carbon dioxide emissions come from burning coal and making cement.

OTHER SOURCES OF CARBON DIOXIDE

Burning fossil fuels isn't the only way people add lots of carbon dioxide to the atmosphere. To clear land for crops, farmers in many countries chop down trees and burn them. This deforestation adds a lot of carbon dioxide to the air. It also removes plants that would naturally take carbon dioxide out of the air for photosynthesis.

Tilling (digging up) the soil on farms releases carbon stored in soil. The carbon rises into the atmosphere as carbon dioxide. Certain industrial processes also add to the problem. For example, making cement releases large amounts of carbon dioxide.

Not all the carbon dioxide that's added to the atmosphere stays there. Some enters other parts of the carbon cycle. Plants absorb carbon dioxide from the air. So does the ocean. But human activities are adding far more carbon dioxide to the atmosphere than natural processes take out.

Fires burn in the Amazon rain forest as land is cleared for cattle grazing.

WHAT'S UP WITH OTHER GREENHOUSE GASES?

Carbon dioxide is not the only greenhouse gas on the rise. Methane and nitrous oxide are rapidly increasing in the atmosphere too. Methane traps twenty-three times as much heat in the atmosphere as carbon dioxide does. Nitrous oxide is three hundred times better at heat-trapping than carbon dioxide.

HOW MUCH IS UP THERE?

So how much carbon dioxide is in the atmosphere? And how fast is it increasing? A U.S. scientist, Dr. Charles David Keeling, started taking very accurate measurements of atmospheric carbon dioxide in the late 1950s. To get the best data, Keeling needed to sample the cleanest air possible. That meant taking measurements far away from cities, highways, and other sources of pollution.

In 1958 Keeling began measuring carbon dioxide from a laboratory on top of Mauna Loa, the highest mountain peak on the island of Hawaii. After just a few years, Keeling had conclusive proof. Atmospheric carbon dioxide was steadily increasing. Every year the amount of carbon dioxide in the atmosphere was higher than the year before.

That trend continues. When Keeling began his work, the level of atmospheric carbon dioxide was about 280 parts per million (ppm). (In every one million "parts" of air,

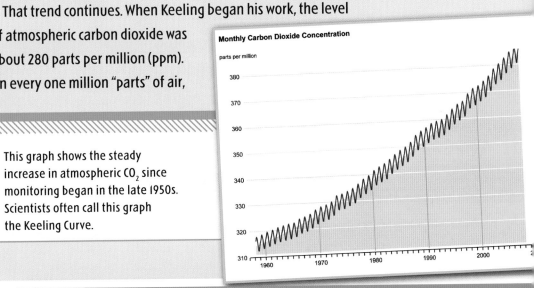

Monthly Carbon Dioxide Concentration

parts per million

This graph shows the steady increase in atmospheric CO$_2$ since monitoring began in the late 1950s. Scientists often call this graph the Keeling Curve.

280 were carbon dioxide molecules.) Since then that level has increased to over 380 ppm. That's more than at any point during the last 650,000 years.

CLUES FROM THE PAST

How do scientists know how much carbon dioxide was in the air long ago? They are able to measure carbon dioxide trapped in ancient ice.

Scientists drill into thick glaciers and ice sheets in different parts of the world. They take out long cylinders of ice. These ice cores contain many thin layers. Each layer represents one year's snowfall. The oldest layers of an ice core are at the bottom. The youngest are at the top.

The layers in an ice core contain tiny bubbles of trapped air. The bubbles are a record of what the air was like the year each layer formed. Scientists can measure the carbon dioxide in these air bubbles. That tells them how much carbon dioxide was in Earth's atmosphere at different times in the past.

FROZEN IN TIME

The longest, oldest ice cores come from very thick ice in Greenland and Antarctica. To date, the longest core ever drilled is from East Antarctica. The core contains layers of ice dating back at least 740,000 years.

This ice core was drilled from Antarctica in 1993. The core was shipped to a laboratory where scientists studied the bubbles trapped in each layer of ice.

By measuring other gases in the bubbles, scientists can also tell what Earth's temperature was. Ice cores reveal that atmospheric carbon dioxide and Earth's average surface temperature are closely linked. The less carbon dioxide in the atmosphere, the lower the temperature. The more carbon dioxide, the higher the temperature. This connection between carbon dioxide and global temperature has held true for hundreds of thousands of years.

CARBON DIOXIDE AND GLOBAL WARMING

Since the Industrial Revolution began, levels of greenhouse gases have increased. So has Earth's temperature. Scientists know this is no coincidence. The link between greenhouse gases—especially carbon dioxide—and global warming is very strong.

In 2007 climate scientists worldwide agreed: Greenhouse gases that human activities are adding to the atmosphere are intensifying Earth's greenhouse effect. They are raising our planet's average surface temperature. And more warming is on the way. Just how much depends on what people around the world decide to do.

NOT JUST MOTHER NATURE

Until the early 2000s, global warming was a controversial topic. Initially many people, including some scientists, thought Earth's recent warming was just part of a natural cycle. For example, the amount of solar energy striking Earth increases and decreases over a period of about eleven years. This variation is due to sunspots. Sunspots are cooler patches that form on the sun's surface. When there are more sunspots, less solar energy reaches Earth and vice versa. Natural cycles such as this do affect global temperature. But nearly all scientists agree that natural cycles alone cannot explain global warming. The evidence is overwhelming that human activities are responsible for most of the current warming.

CHAPTER THREE

EARTH'S CHANGING CLIMATE

So what? What if the world is getting warmer by a few degrees? How much difference could a few degrees make?

In fact, they can make a world of difference. About eighteen thousand years ago, Earth's average temperature was only slightly cooler than it was in the past century. Yet vast glaciers covered large parts of the Northern Hemisphere. In North America, these great ice sheets extended from northern Canada to where Kansas and Oklahoma are.

The glaciers formed because a few degrees of cooling changed Earth's climate. Climate is the average weather a place has over a long period of time. During the time of the glaciers, winters were much colder. Summers were cooler and shorter. More snow fell than melted. Glaciers grew very thick and covered immense areas of land.

Then, very gradually, Earth's average surface temperature increased a few degrees. The ice sheets slowly melted and retreated. By about ten thousand years ago, the only large areas of ice left were on mountain tops and near the poles.

24

The melting ice in Greenland is shown in both of these images. *Left:* A stream of meltwater cascades off part of the Greenland ice sheet. *Below:* Water pours off an iceberg that broke off a glacier in Greenland.

EXTENT OF GLACIERS IN THE LAST ICE AGE

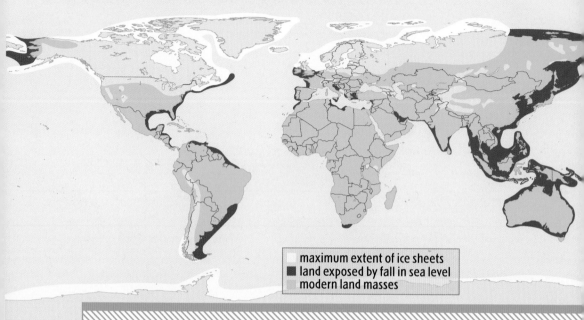

■ maximum extent of ice sheets
■ land exposed by fall in sea level
modern land masses

About eighteen thousand years ago, a cooling of Earth's average surface temperature led to global climate change. Huge sheets of glacial ice covered large parts of several continents. So much water froze into ice that the sea level fell along many coastlines.

Recent global warming is raising Earth's temperature very quickly. Many scientists believe climate will change worldwide in response to this sudden warming. They've found a lot of evidence that it is already changing.

CLIMATE MODELS

When Earth's temperature began rising, scientists wanted to know how that warming might change the climate. They also wondered how climate changes could affect life on Earth.

Climate isn't something you can study under a microscope or in a laboratory. Scientists created models of Earth's climate system. Climate models are very complex computer programs. Scientists build climate models by dividing Earth's surface and atmosphere into blocks, or cells, within the program. Then they develop sets of math equations that describe the conditions in each cell. These equations reflect how temperature, humidity, wind speed, ocean currents, and other factors interact. More equations link all the cells. In that way, they work together as a whole, like Earth's real climate system.

Weather models are a bit like climate models. Meteorologists are scientists who study and predict the weather. They enter current weather data into weather models. Then the models make a projection based on the data. They show, or forecast, what the next few days of weather will be like.

27

CLIMATE VS. WEATHER

Don't confuse climate and weather. Weather is the warm, cold, sunny, or rainy condition of the atmosphere at any given time. Weather changes quickly from day to day. Climate is the typical weather a place experiences from year to year over a long time.

This meteorologist is studying weather projections made by a computer weather model. Climate scientists use climate models to project how global warming will likely affect Earth.

Similarly, scientists use climate models to make climate projections. These are predictions about what the climate may be like in the next decade or century. However, predicting climate is much more complicated than figuring out tomorrow's weather. So climate models are much more complex than weather models.

Making accurate projections of how global warming may change the climate worldwide is enormously difficult. Early climate models were rough. They included the best data scientists could gather at the time. But for some parts of the climate system, data simply weren't available.

By the end of the twentieth century, however, climate models had improved a lot. New satellites and other advanced tools collected much more data. They also collected new kinds of data. Modern climate models are much better at simulating Earth's climate system than earlier versions. Computers that run climate models are faster and more powerful too.

To make climate projections, scientists program a model to test what climate would be like under different conditions. For example, a model could test the effects of carbon emissions decreasing, increasing, or staying the same over the next ten years. How much would Earth warm in each case by the year 2100? How would the resulting warmth change the climate worldwide?

Climate isn't something you can study under a microscope or in a laboratory.

Climate models still aren't perfect. They never will be. But scientists are confident in the projections modern climate models are making. Many predictions have already been confirmed by observations. In other words, what the models are saying will happen has already begun to happen. The following projections and evidence will give you an idea of what has happened already and what may be still to come.

GLOBAL SURFACE TEMPERATURE

Projections

If people worldwide cut carbon emissions drastically and soon, levels of atmospheric carbon dioxide might stay below 400 ppm. That would limit further global warming to about 3.2°F (1.8°C) by 2100. But if people keep burning fossil fuels at the current rate, carbon dioxide levels could reach 780 ppm by 2100. That could raise Earth's temperature by as much as 11.5°F (6.4°C). Our planet would be warmer than it has been in more than one million years.

Models show that different parts of the planet may warm more or less than the global average. All climate models project that places near the North Pole and South Pole will warm the most.

Evidence

Earth's average surface temperature increased 1.4°F (0.8°C) during the twentieth century. The Arctic warmed nearly 5°F (2.8°C) during the same period. The Antarctic Peninsula has warmed almost as much as the Arctic. This finger of land juts out from Antarctica toward South America. All told, Earth is already warmer than it has been during the last ten thousand years.

Melting sea ice breaks up in the Arctic Ocean north of Canada.

OCEAN TEMPERATURE

Projections

Climate models forecast that as the air near Earth's surface warms, so will the ocean. Models also predict that the ocean will warm fastest near the equator. However, water warms more slowly than land or air. The larger the body of water, the slower the change. And the ocean is really big. It covers three-quarters of Earth's surface and is 13,000 feet (4 km) deep on average. So any change in its temperature should be very gradual.

Evidence

Scientists have determined that since the 1960s, the ocean has warmed 0.18°F (0.10°C) from the surface down to about 2,297 feet (700 meters). That may not seem like much. But an enormous amount of heat is needed to raise the ocean's temperature even just a little. And as predicted, tropical ocean waters have warmed more than those nearer the poles.

TAKING THE OCEAN'S TEMPERATURE

In 2000 scientists from several different countries began a project to measure ocean temperature as precisely as possible. The project, called Argo, uses more than three thousand instrument-packed floats. Argo floats *(shown above)* are bobbing on ocean waves worldwide. They measure water temperature and saltiness down to a depth of 6,562 feet (2,000 m).

MELTING ICE

Projections

Models project that as global temperatures rise, sea ice, ice sheets, and glaciers will begin to melt. Melting should be most severe in polar regions. That's because warming there will be the greatest.

30

Melting mountain glaciers will directly affect water supplies in some areas. For example, the Himalaya Mountains have more than fifteen thousand glaciers. Millions of people in several countries, including China, depend on the glaciers' melted runoff for drinking water. Climate models predict that 80 percent of Himalayan glaciers will be gone by 2100. As the glaciers disappear, so will the drinking water.

Evidence

Since about 1978, satellites have been tracking sea ice in the Arctic Ocean. Satellite pictures show that the area covered by ice year-round is steadily shrinking. Melting has increased dramatically since about 2000. Between 2005 and 2007, the year-round ice has shrunk by an area the size of Texas and California combined. And in the summer of 2007, the area covered by Arctic sea ice was the smallest it's ever been. Some scientists think that the ice may completely disappear by the summer of 2013. The ice cap will exist only in winter.

Ice is also melting on the opposite end of the world. Scientists have studied more than 250 glaciers on

These satellite images show recent changes in Arctic sea ice. The image on top shows the sea ice area in summer 1979. The image on the bottom shows the sea ice area in summer 2007.

the Antarctic Peninsula. They've found that since the mid-1900s, 87 percent of the glaciers have melted significantly. On both sides of the peninsula, ice shelves extend out into the ocean. Warmer temperatures are weakening the ice shelves. Several state-sized pieces of these ice shelves have broken off since the 1990s. The massively thick ice sheets that cover Antarctica's interior are also showing signs of melting around their edges.

After Antarctica, Greenland has the world's second-largest ice sheet. But global warming has triggered unexpectedly rapid melting of Greenland's ice. Scientists calculate that since 2006, the island has lost roughly 165 billion tons (150 billion metric tons) of ice per year. That is twice as much ice as is in all the glaciers in the Alps, Europe's largest mountain range.

Glaciers in the Alps are also melting. That's true of most mountain glaciers worldwide. Teams of scientists have reported dramatic shrinking of glaciers in Alaska. Montana's Glacier National Park may have no glaciers left by 2030. Mountain glaciers are also disappearing in Peru, Chile, Nepal, Tanzania, Switzerland, and other countries.

NORTHWEST PASSAGE OPENS!

In the summer of 2007, so much Arctic sea ice melted that open water linked the Atlantic and Pacific Oceans. For centuries, sailors searched for a "northwest passage" that would have made such a boat trip possible. But sea ice always blocked the way. Climate models projected the passage would eventually open as global temperatures rose. But none predicted it would happen so soon.

32

SEA LEVEL RISE

Projections

Sea level is a measure of how much water is in the ocean. Sea level measurements show how high onto land the ocean reaches. All climate models project that global warming will raise sea level worldwide. This sea level rise has two causes. First, as water warms, its molecules spread out. So water already in the ocean takes up more space. Second, when ice sheets and glaciers melt, water that had been stored on land is added to the ocean. This increases the ocean's total volume. The more water that's added, the higher sea level will rise.

Rising sea level will threaten people living on islands and near the ocean. Worldwide, eleven of the world's fifteen largest cities are on a coast. Dramatic sea level rise won't happen anywhere overnight. But it could ultimately force millions, even billions, of people to move to higher ground. Rising seas would also flood thousands of square miles of coastal cropland. And the salt water would contaminate freshwater sources. So fewer food and drinking water supplies will be available.

Evidence

Sea level rose more than 6 inches (15 centimeters) between the late 1800s and 2000. The rate of increase sped up toward the end of the twentieth century. Between 1993 and 2005, sea level rose about 0.1 inches (3 millimeters) per year. If that trend continues, sea level is likely to be 11.2 to 17.2 inches (28 to 43 cm) higher by 2100. But this projection is very uncertain. It all depends on how much land ice melts and flows into the sea. If the entire Greenland ice sheet melts, that water alone would raise sea level by 24 feet (7.3 m). Melting of the Antarctic ice sheets would raise sea level by several hundred feet more.

A scientist measures the ground-level temperature on the tundra in northern Alaska.

THAWING TUNDRA

Projections

The Arctic tundra lies south of the Arctic Ocean. It is an immense, treeless landscape. Typically during summer, only the top few inches of tundra soil thaw. Below that the ground remains frozen. This permanently frozen soil is permafrost. Climate models project that as Arctic regions warm, much of the tundra's permafrost will melt.

Evidence

The climate on the tundra is changing rapidly. Permafrost is melting in northern Alaska and northern Canada. In western Siberia, scientists have discovered that roughly 386,000 square miles (about 1 million sq. km) of permafrost have thawed. If warming continues as expected, 90 percent of the permafrost in all Arctic regions could melt by 2100.

Tundra thawing is more than a problem of soggy ground. Tundra soil is rich in dead plant and animal matter. That means it's rich in carbon. Scientists estimate that worldwide, permafrost holds 992 billion tons (900 billion metric tons) of carbon. As long as the soil is frozen, the dead matter doesn't decay. But as tundra soil melts, decay processes get under way. Melting permafrost is releasing huge amounts of both carbon dioxide and methane from decay into the atmosphere.

MORE SEVERE WEATHER

Projections

Climate models project that global warming will change weather patterns worldwide. As temperatures rise, moderate weather patterns will tip toward extreme weather patterns. Severe storms and heat waves are likely to be more common. Changes in precipitation will increase chances of flooding in some places. They'll bring droughts to others.

Heat waves, droughts, and floods can have serious consequences for people. Because of climate change, at least 75 million people in Africa could face severe water shortages due to drought by 2020. Where African farmers depend on rainfall for their crops, food supplies may drop by 50 percent.

Heat waves and droughts spark wildfires. These fires could destroy large parts of many North American forests in the coming years. More fires will likely threaten cities, especially in drought-prone areas like Southern California. As glaciers disappear in the Rocky Mountains, people in western states may face severe water shortages and more frequent and severe wildfires. In the U.S. Southwest, drought conditions may become permanent. People living in cities there could find it difficult to get enough water. Farmers and ranchers might eventually be unable to raise crops and livestock.

These farmers stand in a parched field in Australia in 2006.

In the future, increased flooding in parts of the world will likely drive millions of people from their homes, at least temporarily. Crops will be destroyed and topsoil washed away. Floods also spread life-threatening diseases.

Evidence

Hurricanes form over warm oceans. The storms draw strength from the heat in surface waters. As the ocean warms, it may spawn more powerful hurricanes. Scientists don't link any individual weather event, including a hurricane, directly to global warming. But several science teams report an increase in the number of powerful hurricanes since the 1990s. Other scientists, however, say the evidence isn't strong enough. More information is needed to determine if global warming is the cause of this increase.

Heat waves do appear to be on the rise. In August 2003, Western Europe experienced its worst heat wave on record. More than thirty-five thousand people died as a result of record-breaking temperatures. In 2006 heat waves struck Europe again, along with the United States. In 2007 unusually severe heat

Young people in Lahore, Pakistan, cool off in a canal during a June 2007 heat wave.

waves blasted India, Pakistan, and parts of Russia. Southeastern Europe and parts of North Africa also roasted in scorching temperatures.

Heavy rains and floods seem to be becoming more common. In 2005 Mumbai, India, received a world-record 37 inches (94 cm) of rain in twenty-four hours. In 2006 in Hawaii, nearly 11 feet (3.4 m) of rain fell on Mount Waialeale in just six weeks. In 2007 record-breaking floods ravaged parts of the United Kingdom, the United States, Indonesia, India, Bangladesh, and Nepal.

Meanwhile, droughts have been increasingly widespread in Europe, Asia, Canada, and parts of Africa since the 1990s. Since 2001 Australia has suffered from the worst drought in its history.

CHANGING SEASONS

Projections

As temperatures warm, seasons will change in many parts of the world. Models predict that winters will be warmer and shorter in many places. Spring will come earlier. Summers should be hotter and last longer.

For people living in Arctic regions, a warmer climate and longer summers will bring great change. As snow and ice melt, people will lose their traditional way of life. In temperate (mild-weather) regions, a longer summer growing season could mean higher crop yields for farmers. Some crops also may grow faster because of more carbon dioxide in the air. But weeds will grow faster too.

THE NENANA ICE CLASSIC

Since 1917 people in the village of Nenana, Alaska, have been betting on the exact minute when spring will arrive each year. The agreed-upon start of spring is the moment the ice breaks up on the nearby Tanana River. For scientists the Nenana Ice Classic, as this contest is called, is a source of data about climate change. Based on event records, spring arrives ten days earlier around Nenana than it did in 1960.

An Inupiat hunter walks on melting sea ice on the Chukchi Sea in Alaska. The Inupiat used to use dogsleds or snow machines for their hunting on the ice. Melting sea ice has forced them to drag boats across patches of ice to open water.

Evidence

Spring snowmelt in the western United States starts roughly a month earlier than it did in the early 1970s. In many northern parts of the country, lakes and rivers thaw several days to a week earlier in spring. In Europe, spring begins one to two weeks earlier than in the 1970s.

ANIMALS AND PLANTS

Projections

Changes in weather patterns and seasons will impact many plants and animals. Models predict that plant populations will tend to move toward the poles. Migrating animals may change the timing of their travels. Or they may change the routes they take to and from their summer and winter homes. Entire populations of animals may also move permanently to escape too-high temperatures. However, not all species will be able to move or move fast enough. These species may not survive. Researchers estimate global warming may drive 15 to 37 percent of North American plant and animal species to extinction by 2050. Some harmful species, such as malaria-carrying mosquitoes, may invade areas where they never lived before.

Evidence

Scientists in the United States recently studied 1,400 kinds of plants and animals. They found that more than 80 percent start their spring activities earlier than they used to. On average, trees bud out, frogs mate, insects hatch, and birds nest more than a week earlier than they did in the 1960s. A 2003 study showed that 1,700 plant and animal species had moved toward the poles. They shifted about 4 miles (6.4 km) per decade closer to the poles over the last fifty years.

In addition, at least twenty-one kinds of ocean fish have left waters that have become too warm. Some moved closer to the poles. Others headed for deeper, cooler water.

NO GOING BACK

Global warming and climate change have the potential to drastically change life on Earth. In the coming years, some of the effects of global warming might not be as bad as models project. But others might turn out to be much worse.

We can't reverse the situation. Earth is already warming. Some degree of climate change is inevitable. But the future isn't set in stone. By acting quickly to reduce greenhouse gases, the world still has time to avoid the worst that global warming might bring.

NATURAL CLIMATE-CHANGING FORCES

Many natural forces shape climate. When volcanoes erupt, they send dust high into the atmosphere. That volcanic dust can block solar energy and slightly cool Earth's surface. Patterns of winds and ocean currents also influence climate worldwide. When these patterns change, so does climate. One such change is the El Niño-Southern Oscillation (ENSO). ENSO is a set of changes in the Pacific Ocean's wind and water. These changes take place every few years. They affect the weather on several continents that border the Pacific. Other forces of natural climate shift are changes in Earth's tilt on its axis or in its path of orbit around the sun. But as with recent global warming, natural forces alone can't explain recent climate change. Human activities are largely to blame.

KLING A GLOBAL
BLEM

Global warming may seem like a new problem. But scientists began raising concerns about it in the 950s. However, people and governments worldwide mostly ignored them.

ONE HOT SUMMER

n the 1980s, Dr. James Hansen, a U.S. climate expert, started speaking out publicly about global warming. He maintained that warming was not just a remote possibility. It was very likely to happen as a result of fossil fuel use worldwide. Hansen testified before Congress in the summer of 1988. He warned that as the world warmed, climate would almost certainly change.

That same summer, the United States suffered a record-breaking heat wave. Both the heat and the issue of global warming made headlines. A number of climate experts called for governments to take action to reduce greenhouse gases. But a few scientists downplayed the problem. So did many government officials and industry leaders. They cautioned that cutting back on using fossil fuels would harm the economy. Industries would shut down. People would lose their jobs. Politicians claimed there was too little evidence to support global warming hypotheses. It was better, they said, not to act.

Left: Dr. James Hansen, shown here in 2006, talks about changing weather patterns. Hansen started speaking out about global warming and climate change in the 1980s. *Below:* A power station rises in the distance behind an open-pit coal mine in Germany.

Concerned scientists didn't give up. They worked with the World Meteorological Organization and the United Nations Environment Programme to establish the Intergovernmental Panel on Climate Change (IPCC). The IPCC objectively reviews research about global warming and climate change. It studies the potential impacts of climate change and ways to reduce those impacts.

THE IPCC

The IPCC brings together hundreds of climate scientists from many countries. The scientists form three main working groups. Each group reviews scientific knowledge of a different aspect of global warming and climate change. The IPCC has published major reports on climate change in 1990, 1995, 2001, and 2007.

42

THE KYOTO PROTOCOL AND BEYOND

Following the formation of the IPCC, several international conferences about global warming took place. In 1992 the Earth Summit, held in Brazil, produced the first international treaty on climate change. This agreement, called the United Nations Framework Convention on Climate Change (UNFCCC), outlined voluntary guidelines for reducing carbon emissions. Nearly

UNITED NATIONS CONFERENCE ON ENVIRONMENT AND DEVELOPMENT
Rio de Janeiro 3–14 June 1992

The Earth Summit in Brazil in 1992 brought world leaders together to talk about climate change.

Members of the United Nations and the IPCC show their latest report on climate change at a conference on global warming in 2007.

two hundred countries signed the treaty. However, few actually followed the guidelines. Cutting emissions required making changes, especially in industries. The changes cost money. Many governments felt they couldn't justify the cost.

The UNFCCC was a starting point. But stronger measures were needed. In 1997 a number of countries approved an addition to the treaty, called the Kyoto Protocol. The Kyoto Protocol legally requires countries to limit greenhouse gas emissions. The Kyoto Protocol gives specific goals for lowering emissions between 2008 and 2012. Most of the world's nations eventually agreed to the Kyoto Protocol. But a few countries, including the United States and Australia, did not. Nevertheless, the Kyoto Protocol went into effect in early 2005. All the participating countries are working to meet their emission goals.

In 2007 representatives from over 180 countries met in Bali, Indonesia, for another climate conference. The conference ended with an agreement by all the participants, including the United States. They agreed to work together on a global plan to address climate change issues by 2009.

European countries have taken major steps in cutting greenhouse gas emissions. The twenty-seven member states that form the European Union set up the Emission Trading Scheme (ETS). It is the first international trading system for carbon dioxide emissions. The ETS sets limits on large carbon dioxide emitters such as coal-burning power plants. If a plant goes over its limit, it must buy carbon credits from other companies (or countries) that pollute less to cover the excess. Typically, plants don't want to spend money buying more carbon credits. So the system encourages them to keep emission levels low. In 2007 more than ten thousand European power plants and other industrial CO_2 emitters were part of the ETS.

CARBON TRADING

Exchanging carbon credits is called carbon trading. It has become a big business. Here's how it works: A company (or country) that goes over its carbon dioxide emission limit can buy or trade for carbon credits from a seller. The seller might be a developing country that emits little carbon dioxide. Or it could be a company that emits less than its limit. Carbon trading is supposed to help reduce carbon dioxide emissions. It's also supposed to encourage use of cleaner energy, such as solar and wind power. Supporters of carbon trading say it is helping to lower emissions. However, critics say the system has too many loopholes and limits need to be stricter.

STATES TAKE THE LEAD

The U.S. government has been slow to tackle global warming and climate change issues. But many states are taking matters into their own hands. Several are leading the way in trying to reduce carbon emissions in the country.

44

In 2003 the Regional Greenhouse Gas Initiative began. It is a carbon credit trading program for power plants in northeastern states. Power plants receive carbon credits that allow them to release a certain amount of carbon dioxide. (Each credit allows for the release of 1 ton (0.91 metric ton) of carbon dioxide.) If a plant releases more carbon dioxide than it has credits for, it must buy additional credits from plants that release less than their limit. Those that break the rules face heavy penalties.

In 2002 California passed a state law to cut greenhouse emissions from cars. The Clean Cars law was the first of its kind in the nation. It imposed stricter fuel economy and emissions standards on new cars.

SOLUTIONS IN CALIFORNIA

California is the world's twelfth-largest greenhouse gas emitter. In 2005 California's Governor Arnold Schwarzenegger proposed bold targets to reduce the state's greenhouse gas emissions. A year later, the California legislature approved the California Global Warming Solutions Act. The act set emissions limits that ensure the state's greenhouse gas emissions are reduced to 1990 levels by the year 2020. Schwarzenegger signed the bill into law in September 2006. Other states are considering similar legislation.

California governor Arnold Schwarzenegger signs the Global Warming Solutions Act in 2006.

But in 2004, automakers sued California over the law. They said that only the federal government can regulate fuel economy and therefore emissions. California fought back. It took the case all the way to the U.S. Supreme Court. In 2007 the Court ruled that carbon dioxide is a pollutant. That meant that California and other states have the right to regulate it. Eighteen other states quickly adopted the Clean Cars law too.

In December 2007, however, the U.S. Environmental Protection Agency blocked California's Clean Cars law. It was an unexpected move, since part of the EPA's job is to help limit pollutants. California, along with a dozen other states and several environmental groups, quickly responded. In 2008 they filed a lawsuit to require the EPA to comply with the Supreme Court's earlier ruling. Stay tuned!

MAYORS MAKING A DIFFERENCE

On February 16, 2005, Seattle mayor Greg Nickels launched the U.S. Mayors Climate Protection Agreement. That was the same day that the Kyoto Protocol went into effect. The idea behind the agreement was to get leaders from all fifty states to reduce greenhouse gas emissions to 1990 levels by 2012. As of 2008, more than eight hundred mayors of cities across the United States had signed on.

Under the agreement, participants promise to work to reduce carbon emissions in their communities to the target levels set by the Kyoto Protocol. They agree to urge the state and federal governments to do the same. And they agree to encourage members of Congress to pass greenhouse gas laws that will create a national carbon trading system.

Governments are slowly addressing the global warming problem. Placing limits on greenhouse gas emissions is a first step. But governments, industries, and individuals can all do more.

Governments are slowly addressing the global warming problem.

Smoke billows out of chimneys at a power plant in Mongolia in 2007. Countries around the world are working on the problem of global warming. Efforts include reducing emissions from power plants.

ATEGIES FOR A STAINABLE URE

Greenhouse gases must be cut as quickly as possible to slow global warming. How can the world do this? For starters, we can use fewer fossil fuels. And we can switch to other sources of energy that don't release carbon dioxide into the air.

IMPROVING ENERGY EFFICIENCY

The world won't be able to stop using fossil fuels overnight. We're too dependent on them for transportation, industry, and electricity. But we can start using fossil fuels more efficiently right away. Using them more efficiently means we'll use less of them while we make the change to other energy sources.

For starters, we can use fewer fossil fuels.

Replacing gas-guzzling cars and trucks with fuel-efficient vehicles is one way to start. Smaller gas-powered cars are growing in popularity. Smaller vehicles are more fuel efficient than larger trucks and SUVs. Hybrid cars use less fuel than strictly gas-powered cars of any size. That means fewer greenhouse gases entering the air. Most hybrid cars are powered by gasoline and electricity from a rechargeable battery. The battery charges as the car

Left: This hybrid vehicle from Mazda can run on either gasoline or hydrogen gas. When hydrogen combines with oxygen from the air, energy is released to power the car. *Below:* The Toyota Prius cars are popular hybrid vehicles on the market. They run on gasoline and battery power.

LIGHTS OUT!

In 2007 Australia passed a law to ban the sale of incandescent lightbulbs nationwide. Australians are replacing their old bulbs with energy-efficient compact fluorescent bulbs (CFLs). CFLs use about 70 percent less electricity than incandescent bulbs. A similar change in the United States would have huge effects. If every U.S. household replaced three of its incandescent bulbs with CFLs, carbon dioxide emissions would drop by 23 million tons (20.9 million metric tons) per year. That's like saving all the emissions from eleven coal-fired power plants!

moves. About two dozen brands of hybrid cars are already on the market. Appliances we use every day run on electricity. Refrigerators and air conditioners, ovens and clothes dryers, and water heaters and washing machines all need electric power. So do lightbulbs. (How many lightbulbs are in your house?) Switching to energy-efficient appliances and bulbs can save a lot of electricity. And that reduces the amount of fossil fuels we use.

ALTERNATIVE FUELS

Alternative fuels can be used as substitutes for fossil fuels. Two alternative fuels, ethanol and biodiesel, are already sold at gas stations. Burning alternative fuels still releases carbon dioxide into the air. But not as much as burning fossil fuels does.

Ethanol is an alcohol-based fuel. It's made from starchy crops like corn, barley, and wheat. It can also be produced from cornstalks and other plant wastes. Most of the ethanol made in the United States comes from corn. Pure ethanol isn't a substitute for gasoline. But ethanol-gasoline blends are common. You probably see one called E10 at gas stations. E10 is 10 percent ethanol and 90 percent gasoline.

E85 is available at this gas station in Wisconsin, right next to diesel and unleaded gasoline fuels.

Another less common blend is E85. It's 85 percent ethanol and 15 percent gasoline. Ordinary car engines can't run on E85. But flex-fuel vehicles (FFVs) can. FFVs run on gasoline, ethanol, or any blend of the two. It doesn't cost much to turn a regular car into a flex-fuel car. Several million FFVs are already on U.S. roads.

Biodiesel is an alternative fuel for cars and trucks that use diesel fuel. It's made from a mixture of vegetable oil and alcohol. In the United States, most biodiesel is made from soybean oil.

ENERGY CONSERVATION

Conserving energy means using less of it. The less energy we use, the fewer greenhouse gases will enter the atmosphere. We can conserve energy by driving more efficient cars and driving less in general. We can avoid leaving lights on when no one's home or turn down the thermostat before going to bed. We can also make conscious choices about other things we do and how we do them.

For example, people have a choice about how to get to school or work. Driving a car is a choice. But it means a lot of greenhouse gases get added to the air. Taking public transportation is a better choice for Earth's atmosphere. True, a bus or train also burns fuel and releases carbon dioxide. But emissions from one bus are better than those of several dozen cars. The most Earth-friendly choice is to walk or ride a bike. It's slower and probably more work, especially if there are hills along the way! But it's a completely emissions-free way to get around.

This city bus uses hybrid technology to run. In addition to reducing pollution, hybrid buses can save city governments money on the cost of fuel.

MAKING A DIFFERENCE

Global warming may seem like a huge problem that only large organizations or governments can solve. But individuals really can make a difference. When Sarah Ferriter was a student at the University of Southern Maine (USM), she wanted to help reduce greenhouse gas emissions. The university's shuttle buses burned diesel fuel. Sarah thought the buses should change to biodiesel. But biodiesel is more expensive than diesel fuel. So Sarah proposed that every student at USM pay a 1 dollar fee per year to offset the cost. Students loved the idea. So did the administration, which simply covered the extra cost with school funds. USM's buses switched to biodiesel. The university uses biodiesel to heat campus buildings too. Just one person brought about this big change.

Reusing and recycling are also easy ways to conserve energy. Almost everything we use, from paper to plastics, requires energy to make. Using something again and again means a new one doesn't have to be manufactured. Recycling materials like plastics, aluminum, and paper conserves oil, natural resources, and forests. Plus, it saves all the energy needed to transform raw materials into finished products. The savings can

53

A pile of newspapers is ready to be recycled.

be huge. For instance, for every 1 pound (0.5 kilograms) of paper that is used on both sides and then recycled—instead of used once and thrown away—2.5 pounds (1.1 kg) of greenhouse gases are saved.

RENEWABLE ENERGY

Conserving energy reduces the use of fossil fuels, which are a limited resource. It buys time in our warming world to develop renewable energy sources. These include solar, wind, geothermal, hydropower, and biomass. Except for biomass, these energy sources don't add carbon dioxide or other greenhouse gases to the air. And because they're renewable, we'll never run out of them!

54

THE POWER TOWER

Spain's PS10 solar power tower began operating in 2007. A total of 624 huge, movable mirrors (called heliostats) concentrate the sun's rays on top of a thirty-five-story tower. There, a turbine drives a generator to produce electricity. When running at full capacity, the power tower will produce enough electricity to run six hundred thousand homes. And all without releasing a single puff of greenhouse gas!

This solar power tower near Seville, Spain, opened in March 2007.

Solar power is energy from the sun. It can be harnessed in several ways. The first is by using solar panels (called photovoltaic cells). These convert the energy in sunlight directly into electricity. Solar panels used to be very expensive. But new kinds are much cheaper and more efficient. They're also thinner, smaller, and more flexible. Solar hot water systems use the sun's energy to heat water. Solar-thermal power stations typically use mirrors to concentrate solar energy, which powers a turbine. The turbine then spins to generate electricity.

Wind power is renewable energy from moving air. Tall wind turbines stand in open spaces, where the wind spins the turbine blades to generate electricity. Giant wind turbines are becoming part of the landscape in many places. Groups of wind turbines are sometimes called wind farms.

Geothermal energy is natural heat from inside Earth. In some places, intense geothermal heat is stored in steam or hot water deep underground. Geothermal energy can run power plants that give off little or no carbon dioxide. In some places, people use geothermal energy to heat buildings directly.

These wind turbines on a wind farm in California supply energy to the Oakland area.

Moving water also has power. (You know this if you've ever paddled a canoe upstream.) Hydropower is energy captured from water flowing along a river or surging out of a dam. The back-and-forth movement of ocean waves is a source of water power too. Waves can drive turbines to produce electricity. So can tides. Tides are the regular rising and falling of the ocean along a shoreline. In some places, changing tides create strong currents. Put a tidal turbine in the water, and the turbine's spinning blades will change the water's energy into electricity.

Electricity from grass clippings and wood chips may sound strange. But those wastes, called biomass, were once parts of plants. The plants captured energy from sunlight and stored it in leaves, stems, and trunks. When biomass burns in huge boilers, the heat that's released can turn water into steam. The steam can turn turbines to generate electricity. Burning biomass does release carbon dioxide. But the amount released is the same as was removed from the air during the plant's lifetime. So biomass is considered a "carbon-neutral" source of power.

56

CARBON-NEUTRAL LIFESTYLES

People can be carbon neutral too. They can try to adopt a carbon-neutral lifestyle. That means taking creative steps to get rid of, or cancel out, everyday activities that generate carbon dioxide.

Dried hay and plant stalks are covered by a tarp and tires outside a bioenergy plant in Germany.

The first step toward a carbon-neutral lifestyle is to calculate your carbon footprint. That's a measure of how much carbon dioxide you put into the air every day. It's usually expressed as tons of carbon dioxide or tons of carbon emitted per year. Businesses, cities, and countries can have carbon footprints too.

Next, you try to offset your carbon footprint. This means doing things that take carbon dioxide out of the air to make up for things that add carbon dioxide to it. Conserving energy can help offset carbon emissions. So can buying carbon credits. Individuals can do this, not just companies and countries. All sorts of projects allow people to purchase carbon credits. Buying carbon credits "retires" credits that would otherwise be traded to countries or companies. Retiring credits makes them harder to get. There are fewer to go around. So it encourages countries and companies to reduce their emissions. That reduction of emissions offsets the carbon footprint of the person who bought the carbon credit.

You can also reduce your carbon footprint by getting involved in environmental projects that help reduce emissions. For example, you can buy carbon credits from an organization that plants trees. The money goes to plant trees that will take up carbon dioxide from the air. The more credits you buy, the more trees get planted and the more carbon is offset.

TOWARD A GLOBAL SOLUTION

Global warming is a global problem. Addressing it requires a global solution. People everywhere must stop adding greenhouse gases to the air. We must find ways to replace fossil fuels with clean, renewable energy sources.

The world has the technology and the creativity to find these solutions. But we have to be willing to make the effort. And we have to take action soon. If we don't, the amount of atmospheric carbon dioxide will keep increasing. Earth's greenhouse effect will keep intensifying. And a much warmer world will be upon us before we know it.

GOING GREEN

WHAT YOU CAN DO ABOUT GLOBAL WARMING

In one way or another, every person on the planet contributes to global warming. And every person needs to help reduce greenhouse gas emissions. That includes YOU!

Take action! Just thinking about global warming may make you feel helpless. But you're not. You can help stop global warming. And you can start today.

Begin with a few easy steps:

- **Switch out incandescent lightbulbs in your home for energy-efficient CFLs.** Start with the lights that are on most often.

- **Don't waste paper.** Recycle it when you're done using it. Use recycled paper made from 100 percent postconsumer waste. (Check the package.)

- **Save even more paper by reading newspapers and magazines online.** Don't print them out.

- **Take showers instead of baths.**

- **Wash your clothes in cold water instead of hot or warm water.** Then dry them on a clothesline instead of in the dryer.

- **Turn off lights whenever you're not using them.**

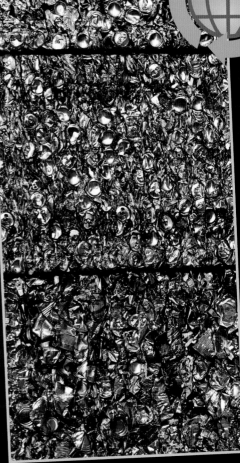

Blocks of crushed aluminum cans lie in stacks, ready to be recycled.

- Plug electronic devices that have a standby mode (such as computers and DVD players) into a power strip. Then turn the strip off when you're not using those devices.

Those weren't too tough, were they? You're ready to move on to a few lifestyle changes. Try some of these:

- Recycle everything you can, from cardboard and cans to plastics.

- If your school doesn't have a recycling program, start one.

- Consume less. Everything you buy has been made using energy. See if you can get a recycled version of the things you need. Try shopping at thrift stores or garage sales. You'll help the planet and save money too.

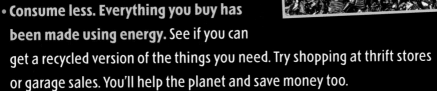

- Buy things that last so you won't have to replace them for a long time.

GOING GREEN

- **Whenever you can, walk instead of riding in a car.** If you can't walk, ride a bike. If you can't ride a bike, take public transportation.

- **Take a reusable bag or tote with you to the grocery store or on any shopping trip.** All those plastic bags are made from fossil fuels. Paper bags are made from trees.

OK, you're on a roll! Here are a few more things you can do that will help a lot to combat global warming:

- **Buy food and other things that are grown or made locally.** Encourage your parents to do this too. Most items in stores come from thousands of miles away. A lot of fossil fuel is burned to get them to your town.

- **Encourage your school or church to reduce emissions.** Start a campaign to raise money for more efficient or Earth-friendly appliances, like a new water heater or solar panels for the roof!

- Calculate your carbon footprint. Several websites, such as the U.S. Environmental Protection Agency (www.epa.gov/climatechange/emissions/ind_calculator.html), can help you do this. Take the time to figure out how you can make your footprint smaller. Then do it.

- Learn more about climate change. Stay informed of what scientists are researching and finding. Tell others what you know about global warming. Encourage them to make Earth-friendly changes too.

Make your voice heard. Write or e-mail your mayor, city council representative, or state legislator. Your letter doesn't have to be long or complicated. Not sure what to write? Here are a few lines that will help you get started.

Dear _____,

Earth is warming because things people are doing are adding too many greenhouse gases to the air. Global warming is changing the planet. It's affecting plants, animals, and people. I'm concerned about global warming, and I need your help in trying to stop it. Conserving energy cuts down on greenhouse gases. I think we could conserve energy by _____.

Thanks. Earth is depending on us.
Sincerely,

_____ Age _____

GOING GREEN

Get involved! Many organizations are working to combat global warming and climate change. Here are just a few you can easily contact:

- **The Alliance to Save Energy**
  http://www.ase.org/
  1850 M Street NW, Suite 600
  Washington, DC 20036
  202-857-0666

- **The Environmental Defense Fund**
  http://www.edf.org/home.cfm
  257 Park Avenue South
  New York, NY 10010
  800-684-3322

- **Natural Resources Defense Council**
  http://www.nrdc.org
  40 West 20th Street
  New York, NY 10011
  212-727-2700

- **Sierra Club**
  http://www.sierraclub.org
  National Headquarters
  85 Second Street, 2nd Floor
  San Francisco, CA 94105
  415-977-5500

Every person can make a difference. That's because small, positive changes do matter. And small, positive changes multiplied millions of times (tell your friends!) produce immense benefits that can truly change the world.

63

GLOSSARY

atmosphere: the layer of gases that surrounds Earth

biomass: plants or plant waste materials that can be used to generate heat or electricity

carbon credit: a credit that a person, company, or country can buy to offset carbon dioxide or other greenhouse gas emissions

carbon cycle: the cyclical process by which carbon moves through the natural world

carbon dioxide (CO_2): an odorless, colorless gas that is a mix of carbon and oxygen; the primary greenhouse gas

carbon footprint: a measure of how much carbon dioxide an individual, group, company, or country produces

carbon neutral: taking in and releasing the same amount of carbon. Biomass is a carbon-neutral power source. People can offset their carbon footprint to become carbon neutral.

climate: usual weather patterns, or the typical weather in a specific region

climate change: a change in normal climate patterns

climate model: a computer model that analyzes climate data to make projections about how climate may change due to global warming

deforestation: the removal of all the trees in an area, usually by cutting or burning

emissions: something sent forth, or released. Released gases that contribute to global warming are called emissions.

evaporation: the process of changing from a liquid into a gas

fossil fuel: a fuel such as oil, coal, and natural gas that formed underground from plants and animals that died millions of years ago

glacier: a large mass of ice in mountain regions that is moving slowly downhill

global warming: the recent warming of Earth's surface and the air just above it, caused by increased carbon dioxide and other heat-trapping gases in the atmosphere. The theory of global warming has been supported by most scientific study.

greenhouse effect: the natural process by which heat is temporarily trapped by the atmosphere rather than radiating directly out into space

greenhouse gas: a name for carbon dioxide and other polluting gases that hold the sun's heat near Earth. These gases cause the greenhouse effect.

ice core: a long cylinder of ice extracted from glaciers and ice sheets

ice sheet: a vast expanse of immensely thick ice on land

ice shelf: part of an ice sheet that extends from land onto water

methane: an odorless, colorless gas; much natural methane is produced by bacteria when dead materials decay; a greenhouse gas

nitrous oxide: a colorless, slightly sweet-smelling gas. Nitrous oxide is a greenhouse gas.

permafrost: permanently frozen soil

photosynthesis: the process by which plants use energy from the sun to convert carbon dioxide and water into sugar and oxygen

photovoltaic: able to generate an electric current when exposed to light

sea level rise: an increase in the average level of the oceans worldwide

solar energy: energy from the sun

sustainable: practiced or used in a way that doesn't destroy or permanently damage a resource

visible light: part of solar energy that human eyes can see

water vapor: a gas that forms when liquid water evaporates

SELECTED BIBLIOGRAPHY

Blackwell Publishing. "North American Birds Moving North as a Result of Climate Change." *ScienceDaily.* June 14, 2007. http://www.sciencedaily.com/releases/2007/06/070611112536.htm (November 9, 2007).

Brahic, Catherine. "Blame for Global Warming Placed Firmly on Humankind." *New Scientist Environment.* February 5, 2007. http://environment.newscientist.com/channel/earth/dn11088-blame-for-global-warming-placed-firmly-on humankind.html (February 13, 2007).

British Broadcasting Corporation. "Climate Changes Shift Springtime." *BBC News.* August 25, 2006. http://news.bbc.co.uk/2/hi/science/nature/5279390.stm (August 27, 2006).

———. "Climate Scepticism: The Top 10." *BBC News.* November 12, 2007. http://news.bbc.co.uk/2/hi/in_depth/629/629/7074601.stm (December 11, 2007).

Conservation International. "Climate Change May Threaten More Than One Million Species with Extinction." *ScienceDaily.* January 8, 2004. http://www.sciencedaily.com/releases/2004/01/040108080103.htm (January 6, 2008).

Coorey, Madeleine. "Australian Drought Linked to Global Warming." *TerraDaily.* April 20, 2007. http://www.terradaily.com/reports/Australian_Drought_Linked_To_Global_Warming_999.html (April 30, 2007).

Dessler, Andrew E., and Edward A. Parson. *The Science and Politics of Global Climate Change.* New York: Cambridge University Press, 2006.

Dow, Kirstin, and Thomas E. Downing. *The Atlas of Climate Change: Mapping the World's Greatest Challenge.* Berkeley: University of California Press, 2007.

Gore, Al. *An Inconvenient Truth: The Planetary Emergency of Global Warming and What We Can Do about It.* Emmaus, PA: Rodale, 2006.

Harrabin, Roger. "China 'Now Top Carbon Polluter'" *BBC News.* April 14, 2008. http://news.bbc.co.uk/2/hi/asia-pacific/7347638.stm (April 14, 2008).

governmental Panel on Climate Change. "Fourth Assessment Report: Climate Change 2007." *IPCC Reports.* 2007. http://www.ipcc.ch/ipccreports/assessments-reports.htm (February 18, 2008).

Office Hadley Centre. "Climate Change and the Greenhouse Effect: A Briefing from the Hadley Centre." *Met Office Hadley Centre Brochures.* December 2005. http://www.metoffice.gov.uk/research/hadleycentre/pubs/brochures/2005/climate_greenhouse.pdf (February 18, 2008).

onal Aeronautics and Space Administration. "The Roles of the Ocean in Climate Change." *NASA: About the Terra Spacecraft.* N.d. http://terra.nasa.gov/FactSheets/Oceans (April 16, 2007).

onal Snow and Ice Data Center. "Arctic Sea Ice Shrinks as Temperatures Rise." *NSIDC Press Room.* October 3, 2006. http://nsidc.org/news/press/2006_seaiceminimum/20061003_pressrelease.html (December 28, 2006).

Center on Global Climate Change. "Climate Change 101: International Action." *Pew Center on Global Climate Change: Global Warming Basics.* 2006. http://www pewclimate.org/docUploads/PEW_Climate%20101%20Intl.pdf (July 7, 2007).

n, John. "Arctic Melt Opens Northwest Passage." *National Geographic News.* September 17, 2007. http://news.nationalgeographic.com/news/pf/38614724 html (April 5, 2008).

Nature Trust. "Melting Permafrost Methane Emissions: The Other Threat to Climate Change." *TerraNature.* September 15, 2006. http://www.terranature.org/methaneSiberia.htm (December 5, 2007).

t, Spencer. "The Discovery of Global Warming." *Center for History of Physics: Online Exhibits.* August 2007. http://www.aip.org/history/climate (August 18, 2007).

d Meteorological Organization. "Top 11 Warmest Years on Record Have All Been n Last 13 Years. *Science Daily.* December 13, 2007. http://www.sciencedaily.com/releases/2007/12/071213101419.htm (April 10, 2008).

FURTHER READING

BOOKS

Cherry, Lynne, and Gary Braasch. *How We Know What We Know about Our Changing Climate*. Nevada City, CA: Dawn Publications, 2008. This book reveals how young people have been involved in research projects that support climate scientists and how readers can do their own research.

David, Laurie, and Cambria Gordon. *The Down-to-Earth Guide to Global Warming*. New York: Orchard Books, 2007. The *Down-to-Earth Guide* is a lighthearted look at global warming and what can be done about it.

Gore, Al. *An Inconvenient Truth: the Crisis of Global Warming*. New York: Viking Children's Books, 2007. Based on former Vice President Al Gore's best-selling book about global warming and climate change, this well-illustrated overview of global warming is appropriate for young adult readers.

Maslin, Mark. *Global Warming: Causes, Effects, and the Future*. St. Paul, MN: Voyageur Press, 2007. Mark Maslin is a climate scientist at University College London in the United Kingdom. He has written extensively about global warming and climate change in books and magazines and for television.

Revkin, Andrew. *The North Pole Was Here: Puzzles and Perils at the Top of the World*. Kingfisher: 2006. This exciting book relates environmental reporter Andrew Revkin's trip to the North Pole, where he worked with a research team studying the relationship between disappearing sea ice and global warming.

Thornhill, Jan. *This Is My Planet: The Kids' Guide to Global Warming*. Toronto, Ontario: Maple Tree Press, 2007. Touching on many different aspects of global warming, this lively book contains suggestions for reducing your carbon footprint, plus several experiments.

WEBSITES

Beat the Heat
http://beattheheat.nrdc.org/
Find out what other people around the country are saying about global warming. Add your own comments to the interactive map.

Climate Connections: A Global Journey
http://www.npr.org/news/specials/climate/interactive/?ps=bb4
This interactive website created by National Public Radio lets readers see and hear about the impacts of climate change on people in many different parts of the world.

EnergyStar
http://www.energystar.gov/index.cfm?fuseaction=popuptool.atHome
Explore an interactive house and learn dozens of ways to save energy on this website, created by the Environmental Protection Agency and the Department of Energy.

Lick Global Warming
http://www.lickglobalwarming.org/
Send a letter to Congress, play a global warming game, and learn ways to combat global warming.

National Geographic Climate Connections
http://ngm.nationalgeographic.com/ngm/climateconnections
National Geographic magazine created this website, where visitors can read articles about climate change and view pictures of its impacts worldwide.

World Wildlife Fund
http://www.panda.org/about_wwf/what_we_do/climate_change/what_you_can_do/index.cfm
This section of the World Wildlife Fund's website gives ways to help slow global warming and climate change. It includes an "Ecological Footprint Quiz" and a link to a carbon footprint calculator.

69

INDEX

71

ABOUT THE AUTHOR

Rebecca L. Johnson is the author of many award-winning books for children and young adults on a wide variety of science topics. She first wrote about global warming and climate change in the 1990s, in her book *The Greenhouse Effect: Life on a Warmer Planet.* More recently, Johnson worked with an international team of climate scientists from the Committee on Earth Observation Satellites (CEOS). They prepared a report outlining the key role of satellites in gathering information about global warming and climate change. The report was presented at UNFCCC climate meetings in Nairobi, Kenya, in late 2006. Johnson lives in Sioux Falls, South Dakota.

PHOTO ACKNOWLEDGMENTS

The images in this book are used with the permission of: NASA , pp. 1 (inset), 3 (top inset), 4-5 (main); © Bill Hauser/Independent Picture Service, pp. 1 (background top right), 3 (background), 9, 12, 26; © iStockphoto.com/MaxFX, p. 1 (background main); © Robert Mann/SuperStock, p. 3 (bottom inset); NASA/GSFC, pp. 4 (inset), 31 (both); © age fotostock/SuperStock, pp. 5, 16, 17; © iStockphoto.com, p. 6; © Maremagnum/Photographer's Choice/Getty Images, p. 7; U.S. Fish and Wildlife Service, p. 10; © David Wrobel/Visuals Unlimited, p. 11 (bottom); © iStockphoto.com/Stephen Sweet, p. 11 (top); NASA/JPL, p. 13; Agricultural Research Service, USDA, p. 14; © iStockphoto.com/Nick Schlax, p. 15; © Jacques Jangoux/Alamy, p. 20; Scripps Institution of Oceanography/UC San Diego, p. 21; © Vin Morgan/AFP/Getty Images, p. 22; © Roger Braithwaite/Peter Arnold, Inc., p. 24; © WorldFoto/Alamy, p. 25; © Scientifica/Visuals Unlimited, p. 27; © Biosphoto/Vernay Pierre/Peter Arnold, Inc., p. 29; Japan Coast Guard/Argo Information Centre, http://argo.jcommops.org, p. 30; © iStockphoto.com/Rafael Ramirez Lee, p. 32; © Gary Braasch, p. 34; © William West/AFP/Getty Images, p. 35; © Arif Ali/AFP/Getty Images, p. 36; © Gilles Mingasson/Getty Images, p. 38; © Jordin Althaus/WireImage/Getty Images, p. 40; © Jorg Greuel/Digital Vision/Getty Images, p. 41; AP Photo/Eduardo DiBaia, p. 42; AP Photo/Fernando Bustamante, p. 43; © iStockphoto.com/Julie Ridge, p. 45 (top); AP Photo/Ben Margot, p. 45 (bottom); © China Photos/Getty Images, p. 47; AP Photo/Yuri Kageyama, p. 48; © Todd Bigelow/Aurora/Getty Images, p. 49; © Todd Strand/Independent Picture Service, pp. 50, 52; © Karen Bleier/AFP/Getty Images, p. 51; © Photodisc/Getty Images, pp. 53, 59; © Denis Doyle/Getty Images, p. 54; © Justin Sullivan/Getty Images, p. 55; © Sean Gallup/Getty Images, p. 56.

Cover: © Berndt-Joel Gunnarsson/Nordic Photos/Getty Images, (top left); NASA (top right); NASA/JSC (bottom right); © iStockphoto.com/MaxFX (background main, type and spine); © Bill Hauser/Independent Picture Service (background top right).

the new book of
Wedding Flowers

simple & stylish arrangements
for the creative bride

Joanne O'Sullivan

⫘ LARK BOOKS

A Division of Sterling Publishing Co., Inc.
New York

Art Director: Megan Kirby
Photographer: Sandra Stambaugh
Cover Designer: Barbara Zaretsky
Cover Photography: www.barberphotography.com
Cover Floral Design: www.nisiesenchanted.com
Assistant Editor: Rebecca Lim
Associate Art Director: Shannon Yokeley
Editorial Assistance: Delores Gosnell
Editorial Intern: Robin Heimer

Special Photography: Sanoma Syndication

R. H. Beck, pg. 99; Dennis Brandsma, pgs. 56, 96; E. Van Lokven, pgs. 46, 141; K. Rutten, pg. 15; J. Van Groenedaal, pg. 80; P. Kooijman, pg. 123; Dolf Straatemeir. pgs. 19, 89, 98, 123; M. Herwig, pg. 132; A. De Leeuw, pg. 124

Contributing Photographers: Allegra's Studio, Artists and Associates, Barber Photography, David Beckstead, Eloise Farr, Lisa Frechette, Audrey Goforth, Robert Marcos, Michael Oppenheim, Arlene Sandler, Parker Clayton Smith, Sandra Stambaugh, Stephen Swain, Unrue Photography, Keith Wright

The Library of Congress has cataloged the hardcover edition as follows:

O'Sullivan, Joanne.
  The new book of wedding flowers : simple & stylish arrangements for
the creative bride / Joanne O'Sullivan.
    p. cm.
  ISBN 1-57990-465-3
  1. Wedding decorations. 2. Flower arrangement. 3. Bridal bouquets.
I. Title.
SB449.5.W4O85 2004
745.92'6--dc22

                              2003022162

10 9 8 7 6 5 4 3 2 1

Published by Lark Books, a division of Sterling Publishing Co., Inc., 387 Park Avenue South, New York, N.Y. 10016

First Paperback Edition 2006
© 2004, Lark Books

Distributed in Canada by Sterling Publishing, c/o Canadian Manda Group, 165 Dufferin Street, Toronto, Ontario, Canada M6K 3H6

Distributed in the United Kingdom by GMC Distribution Services, Castle Place, 166 High Street, Lewes, East Sussex, England BN7 1XU

Distributed in Australia by Capricorn Link (Australia) Pty Ltd., P.O. Box 704, Windsor, NSW 2756 Australia

If you have questions or comments about this book, please contact:
Lark Books, 67 Broadway, Asheville, NC 28801, (828) 253-0467

Manufactured in China

ISBN 13: 978-1-57990-465-4 (hardcover) 978-1-57990-960-4 (paperback)
ISBN 10: 1-57990-465-3 (hardcover) 1-57990-960-4 (paperback)

For information about custom editions, special sales, premium and corporate purchases, please contact Sterling Special Sales Department at 800-805-5489 or specialsales@sterlingpub.com.

ACKNOWLEDGMENTS

Many, many talented designers and photographers contributed to this book. A special thank you to Sandra Stambaugh who handled the local shoot, and our floral design consultants, Stacey Brown and Lynette Dohner of The Bloom Room. Their style, professionalism, and energy were invaluable, plus they're a lot of fun to work with. Thanks also to Shay Brown for all her help at the photo shoot, and for providing props. Rebecca Lim, our assistant editor, pulled together the designer information with persistence, professionalism, and a great attitude. Thanks to Megan Kirby for her beautiful design work and senior editor Paige Gilchrist for all her support and encouragement. Finally, thanks to all the brides who shared their beautiful wedding photos with us!

PHOTO BY WWW.PHOTOGRAPHER.COM

Contents

PHOTOS, LEFT TO RIGHT: WWW.LISAFRECHETTE.COM, WWW.ELOISEFARR.COM, WWW.ELOISEFARR.COM, SANDRA STAMBAUGH

Introduction

Wedding planning is full of so many serious and weighty decisions—from who to invite to whether or not to change your name—that instead of being one of the most joyful endeavors of your life it can be among the most stressful. But, before you start to fret about one more detail of your wedding plan, sit back, take a deep breath, and relax. This part is going to be fun.

Planning your wedding flowers is an exercise in artistry, a chance to indulge your senses and express your style and taste. You don't have to worry about decorum and etiquette, and no one will get their feelings hurt if you chose lilacs instead of lilies. While your mother, sisters, best friend, and fiancé may have a lot to say about the menu or the wording on the invitation, the flowers are safe territory. They may be one of the few wedding details that no one else has a strong (or overbearing) opinion about. So when it comes to flowers, follow your bliss and surround yourself with blooms and blossoms that make your heart sing.

Of course, it's not *quite* that easy—there are a few down-to-earth details you'll have to consider. There's that ever-present budget; the fickle, fragile, *perishable* nature of flowers; and the sheer volume of options to choose from when it comes to bouquet styles, table arrangements, and every other floral embellishment you can think of.

We've put together this book to help you sort through all these particulars, so you can keep your focus on the beauty of the flowers. After all, choosing flowers for your wedding day should be a pleasure, not a chore.

You can use this book in one of two ways.

If you're planning to handle your own flowers, you'll find how-to instructions and advice on carrying out a flower plan on your own. While the art of flower arranging may seem intimidating to the uninitiated, learning to make your own bouquet is a lot easier than learning to make your own wedding dress (and doing it yourself may save you enough money to have that dream dress made for you).

Looking through the arrangements in the book, you'll find that they are refreshingly free of fussiness, which makes them not only beautiful to look at, but easy to recreate.

If you plan to work with a florist, but need to do some research first, use the bouquets and arrangements you see here for inspiration, ideas, and practical advice to help make sure everything stays on track. You'll learn to distinguish orchids from irises, so you'll have a better idea what will complement the feel of your wedding and whether or not your dream flowers are in season and on budget.

If you're not sure which camp you fall into, this book can help you decide. Use the information we provide to weigh the pros and cons of doing it yourself versus working with a florist. You may find that you're not an either/or kind of bride, and decide to take on some of the work yourself while hiring a professional for the rest of it.

No matter what you decide, follow your instincts, choose what you love, and your wedding flowers will certainly be a beautiful part of your perfect wedding day.

Getting Started

PHOTO BY WWW.ROBERTMARCOS.COM

IN THE GRAND SCHEME of your wedding, flowers play more of a supporting role than a lead. While you'll no doubt have some ideas about the look you're going for as your plans progress, you may not get serious about the flowers until you've made a decision on the date, the venue, the dress, the bridesmaids' dresses, and other major considerations. At that point in the process, it's much easier to figure out how the flowers will complement your choices.

A good way to start thinking about the role of flowers in your wedding is by looking at your budget. Once you've got a figure in mind, make a list of all your wedding expenses, from invitations to catering to music. Prioritize the items in order of importance to you. As you think through how to pull off your dream wedding on your very real budget, you'll find out that you're more willing to compromise on some things than others. While there's little chance you'll be able to shave a lot off the cost of your reception site, your flower plan may leave room for flexibility and potentially for savings. There are all sorts of ways to get memorable wedding flowers without breaking your budget. You may work with a florist to figure out how to get the most bang for your flower buck, or you may decide to create the bouquets and decorations yourself. Consider the following points as you decide which route to take.

Do It Yourself & Get Some Help

With an eye on saving money, you may decide to skip the florist and do it yourself. When we say do it yourself, we don't actually mean *yourself*. In addition to having a wonderful fiancé, you probably also have a bunch of wonderful friends who said, "How can I help?" the minute you told them of your wedding plans. And since putting together flower arrangements for the reception is a bit more exciting and glamorous than licking envelopes, you may find that this is one wedding task for which you have more than enough volunteers. Your flower team may include bridesmaids who aren't caught up in other duties, creative friends who have a smaller role in the wedding, or family members. Arranging your own wedding flowers *is* doable—don't let naysayers talk you out of it. But do keep in mind the repetition factor. Making the sixth bouquet is not nearly as fun as making the first one.

If you're nervous about the proposition of undertaking this

task without professional help, consider enrolling in a continuing education class in floral design (chances are there's one at a vocational or community college, garden center, botanical garden, or horticultural society near you). The bonus to taking a class is that, in some cases, you may qualify for a floral design certificate upon completion of the class, making you eligible for floral designer discounts from flower wholesalers. To infuse learning with fun, have a pre-wedding floral design party with your team of helpers. Hire a local floral designer to give you an at-home workshop after hours. This is a fun way to ensure that all your helpers have at least a little experience before they undertake the task of creating your wedding arrangements.

Keep in mind, too, that doing your own wedding flowers is not an all or nothing proposition. After lots of thought, you may decide you don't want to handle your own flowers. That doesn't mean you can't have input. You may hire a floral designer to make the bouquets, but make the table arrangements yourself. You may make your arch or chuppah, but leave the rest to a professional. Getting help doesn't mean relinquishing creative control. You can remain the design director, the arbiter of style, but enlist others to carry out your vision. Of course, you'll want to give the hired designer as much advance notice as possible, especially if you're getting married during the busy season of summer. But if you're asking for only a few arrangements, some florists may be able to fit you in, even if they have other weddings the same day as yours.

Working with a Florist

Before you get too deeply into researching a florist, find out if your ceremony and reception sites will allow you to use your own (some places insist you use one of their choosing). If you do have a choice, the best way to start looking for a florist is by asking friends who understand your sense of style. If you're coming up short on recommendations, look in local bridal publications or ask a wedding consultant or even your wedding photographer or caterer—vendors work with other wedding professionals every weekend, so they're bound to have recommendations.

Once you've narrowed down your choices, make preliminary phone calls. Find out if the florist is available for your wedding date and if he or she charges a consultation fee (you may have to pay for that initial visit). Find out if he or she has a website you can visit for examples from previous weddings—you should be able to tell in an instant if the designer's aesthetic is in line with your own. Do some comparison shopping by interviewing different florists.

When you decide to meet with a florist, bring as much information as you can to help inform the conversation. Create a file with ribbons and fabric swatches from the bridesmaids' dresses and your own, and pictures, pictures, pictures—of arrangements and bouquets you like, of your venue and ceremony sites, even of the tableware or linens you'll use. Try to be as specific as possible with your florist. If frilly and frou frou are your worst nightmare, make that known in advance. If gladiolas remind you of funerals rather than weddings, tell the florist. Let the florist know your budget in advance to avoid misunderstandings later.

You'll need to ask questions about what services the florist provides, too. Ask if you can get detailed lists of the flowers and embellishments that will be used and sketches or even a sample bouquet in advance of your wedding. Find out if the florist knows your venue or will visit it in advance to get a feel for the place. As you provide the florist with more details about your wedding, he or she should provide you with a contract outlining the number and kinds of bouquets and other arrangements that will be provided (including the kind and color of flowers and foliage), and a list of any other fees, such as those for delivery, container rental fees, transporting flowers from the ceremony to the reception, clean up, and sales tax. If you agree on all the fees, you'll need to hammer out other crucial details like delivery time, substitute and alternative flowers, and deposit information. Make sure you have an emergency contact number so you can get in touch with the florist on the day of the wedding.

PHOTOS BY WWW.ROBERTMARCOS.COM

A Wedding Flower Plan

LIKE MOST OF YOUR IDEAS for your wedding, you may have unconsciously been thinking about the flowers for quite some time, informally collecting ideas from books, magazines, friends' weddings, or even your own backyard. Now that your wedding planning is under way, it's time to get down to specifics. One way to get a handle on your flower plan is to take inventory: what people and places need flowers at your wedding? The following section will help jumpstart your thinking about what you'll need.

Personal Flowers

The flowers worn or carried by the wedding party and other family members are called *personal flowers*. When deciding what flowers you need for your wedding, personal flowers are a good place to start. While your guests may overlook your table arrangements or door wreaths, all eyes will be focused on the wedding party (at least during the ceremony), so personal flowers are worth investing your attention and a good portion of your wedding flower budget.

BRIDE'S BOUQUET

Many brides have two bouquets made: one to carry throughout the day and then take home to preserve, and a "tossing bouquet" that goes home with whichever single woman beats out the competition to catch it (if you plan to include that tradition).

For some brides, the bouquet is packed with symbolism and includes flowers that have special meaning: a type of flower carried by her mother in *her* bouquet, a flower that played a big role in her

relationship with the groom, or a flower native to her homeland or region of the country. Often a bride chooses a "signature flower" that dominates her bouquet and is echoed in all the other bouquets and arrangements. For other brides, the bouquet is simply an accessory to complement her dress, like a necklace or earrings (see page 38 for more info on bouquet-dress compatibility).

BRIDESMAID'S BOUQUET

A bridesmaid's bouquet can be a small version of the bride's bouquet or made up of entirely different flowers that complement the bridesmaid's dress. It's no longer necessary for each bridesmaid to be a clone of the others. If you have a maid or matron of honor, you may want to make her bouquet distinctive in some way—it could be slightly larger than the other bridesmaids' bouquets or the flowers may be of a slightly different shade of the same flower, for example. You may choose to use entirely different hues of a single flower for each bridesmaid, such as peonies in pink, white, and red, or you may use ribbons in different textures to make each bridesmaid's bouquet unique.

FLOWER GIRL'S FLOWERS

Your flower girl or girls (if you have them) might carry a basket or paper cone of petals, a mini bouquet, or a "kissing ball" or pomander: a ball-shaped bouquet with a ribbon handle carried over the wrist (see page 37). If you choose a kissing ball, make sure the size is proportionate to the flower girl, and that it's not too heavy for her to carry. Flower girls also often wear a "halo" of flowers in their hair or have flowers pinned to their dresses.

FEMALE FAMILY MEMBERS

Traditionally, important female members of the bride's and groom's families (such as mothers, grandmothers, sisters, or children not included in the wedding party) have worn corsages to honor and distinguish them from other guests. The flowers in the corsage often differ from the flowers in the bouquets, being chosen to match the guest's dress. An alternative to a corsage is a single flower stem or tiny handheld bouquet. To avoid using flowers altogether, some brides offer honored female guests a pin or brooch. You could choose a flower pin (silk, beaded, metal) or something symbolic of your wedding (for example, if you're getting married on the beach, a starfish or shell).

HAIR FLOWERS

From a single flower tucked behind the ear to an elaborate wreath, there are lots of ways to include flowers in your wedding-day hairstyle. A flower-covered veil comb, headband, or hat can echo the feel of your dress, adding just the right finishing touch. Bridesmaids and flower girls often wear flowered wreaths, combs, or headbands, too.

BOUTONNIERES FOR MALE FAMILY MEMBERS

Boutonnieres can be as simple as a single flower tucked into a buttonhole, or a little more elaborate, such as a flower wired to a small bunch of herbs and greenery tied with a handsome ribbon. Single leaves (in vibrant fall colors or interesting shapes or textures), acorns, textured foliage (such as dusty miller or lamb's ear), or even tiny seashells are

PHOTO BY WWW.SERENASTUDIO.COM   FLORAL DESIGN CLEARY CREATIONS

the ring bearer (if you have one), usually wear boutonnieres.

YOUR PRECIOUS POOCH & OTHER PETS

More and more couples are including their pets in their wedding ceremonies, and that leads to decorated dogs. The most common wedding wear for pets is a flower garland. When making the garland, make sure you don't use any berries or flowers that would be harmful if eaten, and that the garland is fit loosely enough that the animal won't harm himself trying to eat it. Obviously you'll want to take it off quickly if the dog is unhappy wearing it.

PHOTO BY WWW.OPPENHEIMPHOTO.COM

WEDDING HELPERS

If you're really feeling generous and inclusive, you may want to provide some sort of personal flower for any wedding helpers you may have—the wedding coordinator, officiant, musician, or ushers. It's a nice way to recognize their role in your wedding.

some interesting alternatives to flowers. The groom's boutonniere may be a mini-sized version of the dominant flower in the bride's bouquet, such as a mini-calla lily or daisy. All the male members of the wedding party, plus fathers, grandfathers, and

alternative bouquets

The bride who's willing to break with tradition may dispense with flowers altogether and carry something entirely different down the aisle.

A bouquet of feathers is a striking choice—it's creative, cost-effective, and definitely different. Beaded flowers, a Victorian tradition, are another option.

For evening weddings, some brides and their attendants now carry candles held in broad-rimmed candleholders. Be careful with this alterna-

tive, though. Scalding hot candle wax dripping down your arm can kill the mood and ruin your dress. A lantern is another (potentially less hazardous) way to get the same effect.

Chinese paper parasols are a creative choice for an outdoor wedding under the strong sun. The bridesmaids seem to float gracefully down the aisle, and they stay cool and comfortable, too.

On a hot summer day, bridesmaids may carry beautiful silk or paper fans down the aisle instead of bouquets. This prevents unsightly wilted flowers and keeps the bridesmaids cool at the same time.

Tiny silk purses filled with real or paper flowers are a new trend in bridesmaids' bouquets. If the flowers are real, a watertight container is hidden in the purse to keep the flowers fresh all day.

PHOTO BY WWW.OPPENHEIMPHOTO.COM

Ceremony & Reception Flowers

Now that you know who needs flowers, turn your eye to your ceremony and reception sites. Where do you want to see flowers on your wedding day?

CEREMONY FLOWERS

Flowers at your ceremony help set the mood and let guests know they've left behind the ordinary and entered a special place. The nature of your ceremony and its location will obviously dictate your flower scheme. At an outdoor wedding in a garden in bloom, nature takes care of almost everything, so you may not need any additional flowers. At a cavernous church or giant empty loft, flowers will make the space feel warm and personal. Once you've decided on the location for your ceremony, find out if there is a flower policy. Some churches, temples, or event spaces have a staff person assigned to flowers and don't allow couples to bring in their own arrangements. The venue chooses the arrangements for the day, then charges the fee to the overall bill, or splits the fee among the couples getting married that day. Other venues may simply have a staff person on hand to help you with setup, while still others will leave everything up to you. It's best to find out your venue's policy before getting too far into planning.

Entryway

An arrangement on or over the door to the ceremony site is a nice way to define the space, welcome guests, and set the tone for your wedding. A door wreath, garland, or even a flower-filled bucket or other container hung over the door handle is a memorable detail to consider.

Aisles

You may be walking down an actual aisle or creating one in an open space. Either way, you can create an aisle of flower petals (the more the better) or let your flower girl do the work as she walks before you.

PHOTO BY WWW.BARBERPHOTOGRAPHY.COM

Altar Area

If there's no obvious "altar" space at your ceremony site, you may want to create one by using a flower-covered arbor, arch, or canopy. The flowers in this area will echo the overall feel of your wedding. A single orchid in a ceramic vase is the perfect choice for a Buddhist ceremony table, while a big, formal church wedding may call for towering urns of cream-colored roses. Obviously, you'll want to position any arrangement so that your guests will see it.

Seat or Pew Ends

If your ceremony site needs a little more embellishment, consider an arrangement on pew or chair aisle ends. Something as simple as a large single flower tied with a ribbon may be all you need for an informal wedding. For more formal ceremonies, you may use kissing balls (see page 37) tied with velvet ribbons, or even more elaborate arrangements. Some brides mark only the aisles reserved for family members with a floral arrangement.

RECEPTION FLOWERS

Like your personal flowers and ceremony flowers, the flowers at your reception will help to set the tone for the celebration. Guests spend more time at the reception than at the ceremony, so your reception arrangements will have an impact. Don't feel that the flowers at your reception have to match the bridesmaids' dresses or even your bouquet. It's more important that they look at home in your reception site. Contrast the color of the walls with the color of your table arrangements. If you're outdoors, use interesting containers that will call attention to the arrangements as they compete with the natural surroundings. If you've got a small budget, substitute fruit, candles, minilights, or lanterns for flowers.

Entry Table or Guest Book Table

If there's one spot where a big, showy arrangement is appropriate, it's the entry table. Since this is the spot where table assignment cards or guest books are often placed, it's a good way to catch guests' attention.

Buffet Table

At a buffet table, the guests are really there for the food, not the flowers. Still, it's a focal point at the reception site. First and foremost, you'll want to avoid clutter, so create two or more small arrangements, raised on platforms above the food, instead of one. A great alternative is to use a garland, which hangs in front of the table and doesn't get in the way.

Guest Tables

Guest table arrangements should either be low enough to talk over, or rise higher than eye level so as not to interfere with conversation. A single arrangement in a container is one way to go, but several single flowers clustered in different containers or lined up in a series is a great alternative. You may also leave a single flower or a small bunch or flowers or herbs on top of each napkin or plate in addition to, or as an alternative to, a table arrangement.

Chair Backs

A single flower or small arrangement tied to the back of the guest chairs is a nice detail. If you don't have the time or money to decorate each chair, reserve this special honor for the bride's and groom's chairs.

Tent Poles

A bare pole in a giant tent is an opportunity for garlands, hanging lanterns, or strings of minilights.

Bar

Again, guests are there for the drinks, not the flowers, so don't overdo it. A few petals scattered on the bar are fine, or try a functional and beautiful arrangement—herbs frozen inside shapely bottles are gorgeous to look at and substitute for ice (see below).

PHOTO BY WWW.LISAFRECHETTE.COM

Cake & Cake Table

Your cake designer may take care of it for you, but if not, try to make the cake and cake table look special by scattering petals around or using fruit, such as grapes, berries, lemons, or limes for embellishment.

Send Off

To avoid being pelted with rice or birdseed, couples may provide their guests with flower petals to shower over them as they leave the reception. They're easier to clean up, don't cause undue bodily injury, and make for great pictures.

PHOTO BY WWW.ELOISEFARR.COM

PHOTO BY WWW.GOFORTHPHOTO.COM

Picking Your Flowers

NOW THAT YOU'VE GOT your flower fantasy plan in mind, from bouquets to buffet tables, you'll need to figure out how to get the flowers out of their beds and into your hands.

There are plenty of ways to access the flowers you need for your wedding—the following section will outline your options. Before you read on though, keep this advice in mind: have a backup plan. Flowers are fragile and susceptible to all manner of accident and injury. An early frost, violent windstorm, clumsy courier, or any number of disasters natural or otherwise can leave your peonies petalless, your cosmos crushed, and your snowberries shriveled. Regardless of whether your flowers come from your backyard or are flown in overnight from Thailand, you need to be prepared to make substitutions. Be flexible and open to alternatives. Try to have on hand at least 10 percent more flowers than you think you'll need to

make up for the ones that die or get damaged on the way to your wedding. Despite the best-laid plans, you may end up with dahlias rather than orchids on your table, but they'll look just as beautiful.

Another important point to keep in mind: it's true that you can order many flowers year-round or out of season, but there's a caveat. You can expect

to pay about 25 percent more per stem for an out-of-season flower. Try to stay in-season as much as possible: your flowers will be fresher and cheaper.

BUY FROM A FLORIST
The most traditional way to get your wedding flowers is to order them from a florist, whether he or she is assembling your flowers or not. Florists are bound to have good connections with

wholesalers, and will quickly and easily be able to tell you whether or not what you want is available. A florist will also have the professional experience to advise you on the particular types of particular flowers (Black Magic roses versus Ecuadorian), and the durability and cost of your flowers. Give your florist as much advance notice as possible, and be aware that some of your requests may not be available at the last minute. If you plan to get married on Valentine's Day or Mother's Day weekend, for example, be aware that popular flowers such as roses may be more expensive, or may sell out quickly (again the argument for a backup plan).

BUY DIRECT
FROM LOCAL GROWERS

A great alternative to a florist is to buy your flowers directly from a local grower. While you will be limited to local, in-season flowers, your flowers will arrive straight from the field, which guarantees they'll be fresher and have a longer life than those shipped from far away places. When you begin your planning, go to your local farmer's market to research flower farms in your area. Many farmers who grow produce have flower fields on the side for extra income. Check to see if there's a community-supported agriculture (CSA) farm in your area or a local organic grower's association. They probably know of small farms with flower fields.

BUY FROM ONLINE GROWERS
& RETAILERS

If you can't find a flower farm in your area, you can get flowers delivered to you in "grower's bunches," directly from the growers in other areas. There are

fresh flowers

One way to ensure perfect flowers on your wedding day is to choose flowers that are at exactly the right stage of bloom.

When choosing flowers, look for buds that are just beginning to open. You should see some color coming out from under the leaf sheaf.

If the flowers are too tightly budded, they may never open, and if they are in full bloom when you buy them, they'll fade or lose their petals too quickly.

plenty of online flower sources to check into. Many of them specialize in certain types of flowers, so check out their websites to find a retailer that suits your needs. You may even be able to convince an online wholesaler to sell to you at wholesale prices.

BUY FROM A FLOWER MARKET

If you're lucky enough to live in a city with a flower market, it's a great place to buy your flowers directly. The caveat is that you'll need to arrive at the market early, *really* early (like 4:00 am) to get the good stuff. Some markets will sell only to certified florists, so you will either need to get that certificate (see page 11) or bring a florist with you. Generally, flower markets open to the public later in the morning, but at that point the flowers have been picked over by the professionals. Do a practice run a few weeks before your wedding to talk to the vendors and get advice about what will be available on your wedding day and how you can go about getting it.

GROW YOUR OWN

If you have enough time and enough garden space, try growing at least some of your flowers in your own garden (or your parents' garden). Fall is the perfect time to plant tulips, daffodils, or other bulb flowers for your spring wedding. Have a bulb-planting engagement party and plant hundreds of bulbs—your friends will feel a special connection to the flowers when they see them at your wedding. Of course, this plan can be a little hit or miss. It works best when you know the cycle of your garden (and even then, there's the unpredictable frost that can spoil your plan). A more reliable alternative is to force bulbs indoors during the winter for use at your late-winter or early-spring wedding. Bulb plants like hyacinths make great table arrangements, which you can give to guests to take home. For a late-summer wedding, you can always count on the sunflower to show up, so it's a reliable choice when growing your own.

UNEXPECTED SOURCES

Flowers can be found in unexpected places. Once you step outside the world of wedding-oriented businesses, you're likely to save money.

If you've got a gourmet supermarket in your area, check out its floral department. You might be surprised at the variety of flowers available (from orchids to stock) at affordable prices. Even a regular supermarket might carry rose bouquets and some other common flowers, and discount clubs frequently offer large bunches at small prices. Head to your home improvement center for potted annuals or perennials that can be used as table arrangements—you can use the money you save on flowers to buy interesting containers, then replant the flowers and enjoy them for months after the wedding.

tips

Try to pick up your flowers on Friday (or even Thursday) for a Saturday wedding.

When transporting flowers, keep them in water and surround the heads with tissue paper or newspaper to protect them.

Do It Yourself

If you decide to make some or all of your own wedding floral arrangements, you'll need some instructions and a bit of practice. In this section of the book, you'll find all the information you need to get started.

First, we introduce you to the supplies floral designers use in their work. They're very inexpensive and easy to find, so you won't have to invest a lot of money. You'll also find information and ideas on embellishments—the little extras that florists use to make a design distinctive. There's a quick but useful tutorial in floral design to aquaint you with some basic principals that will help you achieve the look you're after.

When you're ready to begin, you'll find a guide on conditioning flowers of all types, ensuring that your flowers will look their best as long as possible. All flower arrangements start with conditioning, so this is a step you can't skip.

Next is the reference section on techniques. We'll show you how to create all the basic types of wedding flower arrangements—a boutonniere, bouquet, kissing ball, flower girl halo, wreath, garland, and table arrangement. Once you know these techniques, you can adapt or alter the essential elements to create a design of your own, or to recreate the featured designs in the book. There's also some background information on wedding cake flowers and a section on preserving your wedding flowers.

Supplies

YOU DON'T HAVE TO invest in many supplies to make your own wedding bouquets and arrangements, and the ones you *will* need aren't very expensive. You can find most of them in the floral department of craft stores, while others can be found at home and garden stores.

GENERAL SUPPLIES

Knife. A sharp, clean, all-purpose knife will come in handy for cutting, slicing, and scraping flower stems.

Clippers. For cutting through tough stems and twigs, you need a pair of heavy-duty clippers. Lighter clippers are good for detail work, such as nipping dead blooms.

Scissors. Household scissors can handle some of the same jobs light clippers are made for. They're also what you need for cutting ribbon, raffia, string, and other items you might use in your arrangements.

Gloves. If you'll be working with roses at all, have a pair of gloves on hand to protect yourself from thorns.

Floral tubes/water picks. Floral picks and stems are used to keep flowers hydrated. They can be hidden in a vase (with each stem positioned in its own individual tube) or even in a bouquet. Often flowers are kept in tubes until they're ready to be used, then removed. If you need more height in an arrangement, flowers can be inserted into tubes that are then driven into floral foam (this will raise the level of the flower head).

Floral tape. Use this waterproof tape, available in green, brown, white, and clear, to wrap stems or boutonnieres, secure floral foam to the base of a container, to create a stem-holding grid across the mouth of a vase, or for any other simple adhering of one part of an arrangement to another.

Floral wire. You can straighten stems or bind one flower to another almost imperceptibly with thin floral wire. It's used for wreaths and garlands to secure foliage and flowers to a form or to twine. You can also use heavy-gauge floral wire as a base for a flower girl halo (see page 41).

Rubber bands. These are used to bind the stems of bouquets at the bottom. The rubber band is then covered up with ribbon.

Clockwise from bottom left: floral picks, floral tape, stem wire, flower stems, stephanotis stems, clippers, scissors, floral wire, twine, and large clippers

Stephanotis stems. Special stems with cotton heads, which are soaked in water, are used specifically to fit through the center of the delicate stephanotis (called "the wedding flower"). Since real stephanotis stems are too fragile to stand up to use in a bouquet, these artificial stems allow the blossoms to be used and keep them hydrated.

Twine. Twine is used as a base for garlands (see page 40) and to bind bouquets together at the top of the stem, just under the flower heads (see page 34). It comes in many different strengths (look for one that's strong enough to hold, but not so thick that it shows from underneath a satin ribbon).

SUPPLIES FOR ARRANGEMENTS
Floral foam. Floral foam can be used wet or dry. In its dry form, it's placed inside a container and used to keep flowers in place. In its wet form, it's used to keep flowers hydrated in bouquets, arrangements, kissing balls (see page 37), or wreaths. To saturate the foam with water, put it in a container of water, letting it absorb the moisture naturally. It's fully saturated when it sinks and air bubbles stop rising to the surface. This usually takes about 30 minutes. Don't oversoak your foam, or it may disintegrate. For arrangements in vases or other containers, use direct immersion in water as your first choice and floral foam as your second choice (the flowers will last longer soaking directly in water).

Chicken wire. Chicken wire (available at hardware or craft stores) is often used wrapped around wet floral foam to keep the foam from breaking off. It's also used in vase arrangements to provide a grid of support for flimsy stems.

Glass marbles. Used as a decorative touch at the bottom of clear vases or containers.

Flower frogs. Frogs are placed in the bottom of a container and used as a support system for stems. They're best used when you want a somewhat tight arrangement, or when the rim of your container doesn't provide enough support for your flowers. You can find frogs in glass with holes, or in metal with spikes, deep wells, or thick metal mesh.

Spanish moss and sphagnum moss. Used to fill out vase arrangements.

Wire wreath form. Wreaths can be made several ways, but using a wire wreath form is a convenient choice. The form is lightweight, and comes in several different sizes. Alternatives to a wire wreath form are grapevine wreaths or vines that can be shaped into a wreath, or floral foam wreath forms (which can become heavy and break apart when soaked in water and filled with heavy flowers).

From left to right: Spanish moss, clear glass marbles, frog, floral foam ball, chicken wire, wire wreath frame, sphagnum moss, floral foam

Embellishments

A GORGEOUS BOUQUET of flowers is a thing of beauty on its own, but even the most stunning bouquets benefit from a few embellishments for a finishing touch.

RIBBON

One of the great things about hand-tied bouquets is that you get to dress the stems of the flowers in beautiful ribbon to complement the bride's and bridesmaids' dresses. When it comes to ribbon, you've got a lot of choices, from simple double-sided satin to lush velvet or organza ribbon. The color, width, and texture of your ribbon will affect the overall level of formality of your bouquet. A shiny wired ribbon will dress up the bouquet (or wreath, garland, or kissing ball), while a cotton ribbon or piece of raffia or cocoa fiber will give it a more casual feel. Patterned ribbons, such as gingham or toile prints, will give a bouquet a classic country wedding feel. A wired ribbon can be shaped into stiff bows, while a flexible ribbon can flutter loosely at the sides. You may even use a piece of fabric left over from your wedding gown as a ribbon for a perfect match.

If you're looking for something different (and the "something old" for your wedding ensemble), try to find vintage ribbon at flea markets and antique stores—you'll find beautiful textured ribbons in unusual colors that you can't find in most fabric stores. You may even use an antique handkerchief (especially one that has sentimental value), either as a ribbon or tied into your bouquet.

Classic but distinctive, this rose bouquet was wrapped with iridescent wired ribbon. At the top, the ribbon was folded under to resemble a collar of leaves, and beaded inserts were added for extra sparkle.

BEADED INSERTS

For a bit of shine amongst the flowers, beaded inserts (see above, left) are a charming touch. They can be wired into your bouquet or poked through the centers of blossoms to look as if they're growing out of the flowers.

VELVET LEAVES

Velvet leaves (again, see above left) add a beautiful bit of texture to a bouquet, especially a dainty posy. They can be tucked around the edges of the bouquet before it's wrapped up as substitute for real foliage.

CORSAGE PINS

Pearl- or rhinestone-tipped corsage pins add a polished look to bouquets, and are often used in the centers of flowers such as stephanotis, or to attach a boutonniere to a lapel. Most pearl-tipped corsage pins are white, but you can also find them in different colors, such as pink or gray. If your wedding will be held at the beach, try hot gluing a seashell to the tip of a corsage pin as an alternative boutonniere (see above right). This same trick can be applied to other theme weddings: an acorn for a fall outdoor wedding, etc.

Floral Design 101

FLORAL DESIGN IS AN ART, so to a degree it's instinctive. As an art form, it's also highly personal. A design that delights you may leave someone else cold. The trick to designing your own wedding flowers is to combine the basic concepts of floral design with your own sense of style. While you may not have time to become a master designer before your wedding, you can learn just enough to make a few beautiful arrangements and bouquets.

Do a little reading from the following guide, then do a lot of experimenting with flowers and containers—this is a hands-on endeavor that's best learned by doing. Get to know flowers and their idiosyncrasies. Observe them over the course of several days to find out the effects of heat, light, and water on their "vase life." Try combining different foliage with a single type of flower to see what effect the change creates. You'll be surprised how much you can do with just a little experience, and you'll feel more confident as you approach the big day.

Design Basics

All floral designs, from bouquets to table arrangements, are a composite of four basic elements: color, shape and texture, and proportion. Each element needs to be considered concurrently when designing.

COLOR

While you may not have looked at a color wheel since elementary school, it's helpful to review color theory before trying your hand at floral design.

Primary Colors
Red, blue, yellow

Secondary Colors
Green, orange, violet

Tertiary colors
Turquoise, indigo, purple, scarlet, gold, and lime green

Colors opposite each other on the color wheel (such as yellow and violet, blue and orange, green and red, or lime green and purple) are known as *complementary* colors. They create a pleasing contrast when placed side by side.

Colors next to each other on the color wheel (such as scarlet red and red-orange) are called *analogous* colors and create a harmonious look when placed next to each other.

As you move around the color wheel, you can play with the level of contrast and harmony.

Pairing bright green lady's mantle with zinnias in hot colors makes a strong color statement.

The harmony of the colors in this bouquet allows texture to be the star.

Lofty branches of cherry blossoms in a glass cylindrical vase are in perfect proportion.

Red and green are complements, so using them together makes a perfect contrast. But if you move away from red, closer to green, you'll add more harmonious tones to your arrangement. The contrast between orange and green is less, the harmony greater. Moving even closer to green gets you to yellow, then yellow-green, an analogous color.

The effect of color in your bouquet will be influenced by placement and proportion. For example, will you use three orange flowers amidst a bunch of foliage, or just one? In general, it's better to use more than one flower of a certain color to create more impact. If you're intimidated by mixing colors, try making a monochromatic bouquet or arrangement (see pages 50 to 89) and experiment with textures instead.

SHAPE & TEXTURE

Consider the shape of your flowers: are their stems tall and slender, or short and delicate? What about the flower head—is it heavy and compact, or are there several blooms spread out over a stem? Are the petals delicate and papery or smooth and waxy?

Like color, you can use shape and texture to create harmony or contrast. Compact flowers, such as roses, are harmonious in tight arrangements; loose flowers, such as delphinium, harmonize when paired with other loose flowers. To contrast, add a ball-shaped flower, such as a chrysanthemum next to a spiky one like a liatris, or a smooth-petaled flower like a tulip near a ruffly one like a peony.

PROPORTION

The size and scale of your arrangement or bouquet is another key element. Are you going for a delicate or substantial look? Will one arrangement suffice, or do you need multiples? The key to proper proportion is balance. That doesn't mean that you can't put a single strong flower in a dainty vase (that can be a strong statement in contrast). What it does mean is the size, scale, and composition of your elements should complement each other.

In general, floral designs follow basic shapes: circles, triangles, squares, or rectangles. If your design stays within the confines of one of these shapes, it should look harmonious. Avoid a top-heavy or bottom-heavy look—a big bunch of giant sunflowers in a petite vase looks as if it will topple over, just as petite blooms get lost in a big dramatic urn unless you add taller flowers to balance them out.

Your composition doesn't have to exist within one container. Small bunches of flowers in a cluster of tiny vases look sweet. A series of single flowers in bowls or vases is a modern look. On the other hand, a big, bushy arrangement in a giant urn can be just the statement you need for an entry table.

Conditioning Flowers

TO GIVE YOUR WEDDING flowers the best chance of making it through the day without a meltdown, get them off to a good start. Proper conditioning can add days to the life span of a flower, preventing premature wilting and drooping. The process you use to condition a flower varies based on the consistency of its stem (woody, hollow, soft stem, or firm stems) and on the flower's place of origin (did you pick it in your own garden, or has it flown halfway around the world before you met?). All flowers, regardless of the type, will need to drink plenty of water to stay fresh, and most benefit from flower food, too. Check the following section for pointers on how to make sure your flowers look their best on your big day.

FLOWERS FROM YOUR GARDEN

If you'll be harvesting flowers from your own garden, cut them in the cool of the early morning or late evening. Cutting flowers in the hot midday sun can lead to quick dehydration. Plunge the flowers into water immediately, and don't leave them in a hot place or in direct sunlight. Let the flowers soak in tepid water for as long as you can to make sure they absorb as much water as possible.

When you're ready to arrange the flowers, remove the lower leaves (or all of them if it suits your design) and damaged petals. Clean the leaves with a paper towel if necessary. Use a sharp knife to recut the stems at an angle at least 1 inch (2.5 cm) from the bottom. Before you cut further, make sure that you're cutting an appropriate length for your container or for the desired stem length for your bouquet. Once you've cut, you can't put the stem back. If you do cut too much, you may be able to add height by placing the flowers in a block of floral foam or a frog before adding them to your chosen container. When recutting flowers, try to hold them underwater so that more water goes up the stem. Add flower food or just a crushed-up aspirin to your container water, and let the flowers sit and soak in a cool spot. Some flowers benefit from an occasional spritz of water, but you should avoid getting water directly on the petals of others (check with

a florist to find out which ones). Wrap the flowers in cellophane or plastic bags to protect them if you're not going to be using them until the next day (but be careful not to crush the petals).

FLOWERS FROM A FLORIST

Chances are your florist will have already conditioned the flowers for you, but when your flowers arrive, you'll still want to do a little prep work. They may be three to five days old already when you get them. Remove foliage and damaged petals. Recut the flowers (holding them underwater while you do, if possible) about 1 inch (2.5 cm) from the bottom. Your florist will probably provide you with flower food to put in the container water.

WOODY STEMS

If you're using branches from trees or flowering shrubs (such as roses, dogwoods, or cherry blossoms) in arrangements, you'll need special conditioning for best results. Start by bending the stem about 1 inch (2.5 cm) from the bottom until it splits. Scrape the bent area with a sharp knife in a dragging motion. This

removes a good deal of the bark, exposing the interior stem and allowing more water to enter the stem. Next, fill a container with about 2 inches (5 cm) of boiling water. Leave the stems in the boiling water for a few minutes, then dump it out and fill your container with cold water. Let the flowers soak in the water for at least two hours, if possible.

STEMS WITH MILKY SAP

Some stems release a milky sap when cut, so they'll need to be "heat sealed" to stay fresh. To do this, cut straight across the bottom of the stem with a sharp knife, then hold the stem over the flame of a lighter until it starts to burn. This will stop the sap from running.

HOLLOW STEMS

For flowers with hollow stems, such as amaryllis, delphinium, and calla lilies, you'll need to follow a special conditioning routine. Once you've cut the stem at the bottom, invert it. Fill the stem with tepid water, then plug the bottom of the stem with a cotton ball. Let the flower stand in a bucket of water for as long as possible.

SOFT STEMS

Delicate flowers with soft stems should be conditioned with deep, warm water (up to their necks) overnight. Once you've cut your flowers, let them sit in about 2 inches (5 cm) of warm water for about five minutes. Next, fill the container about one-third of the

way up with cold water. This will help the water move up the stem.

FIRM STEMS

Flowers with firm stems like mums and orchids can be conditioned with warm water following the same process used for those with soft stems.

DAMAGE CONTROL

If your flowers start to droop and fade, try a little first aid before giving up on them. Use a hot-water treatment to counteract drooping. Place the stem in a supportive container with 2 inches (5 cm) of very hot water in the bottom. After five minutes, add cold water and flower food to the container. Recut the stems.

conditioning at a glance

Remove any dead flowers or unnecessary foliage first—leaves submerged underwater can start to rot.

Keep your containers clean. The bacteria in a vase can cause premature wilting. Use a bottle-brush to clean, if necessary.

Most flowers do better if they're kept in cool places out of direct light. Likewise, cool water helps maintain freshness.

Don't cut flowers for a vase until you know what size vase you're using. Hold the flower up to the vase first to determine where to cut.

Use a sharp knife, scissors, clippers, or pruning shears to avoid damaging the stems.

Cutting flowers at an angle and using a scraping or dragging motion prepares them to absorb the maximum amount of water.

Add flower food and a few drops of bleach to your water to nourish it and prevent bacteria and fungus from growing.

For arrangements, change the

water every few days if the arrangements have to be made in advance or are to be used after the wedding.

Some floral designers like to spray an arrangement with a preservative after it's done, or add a "leaf shine" product to leaves and foliage to enhance the texture.

Techniques

The step-by-step instructions you'll find in this section will help you to create all of the bouquets or arrangements in the book. Just adapt the instructions to your choice of flowers and add your own creative touches.

Wiring a Flower

In the past, most bridal bouquets were made entirely of wired flowers. Large elaborate bouquets held in thin bouquet holders necessitated the use of wired flowers for dramatic effect. Nowadays, more natural, hand-tied bouquets are in vogue, which means less time spent assembling bouquets and, consequently, less labor time charged to the bride. There are still several situations that require wired flowers, though, so it's useful to know how it's done.

Flowers are wired for two reasons. The first is to strengthen a stem that would otherwise become too weak and flimsy. Nature didn't intend for stems to be positioned into bouquets, so in order to exist in such an unnatural position, the stem needs extra support. A wire is wrapped up and down the length of the stem, then the stem is covered in green floral tape to conceal the wire. This technique is often used for flowers with heavy flower heads, such as sunflowers, roses, gerbera daisies, and orchids.

The second reason for wiring is to create an artificial wire stem for a flower when the real stem needs to be removed to accommodate the floral design. The natural stems are cut off and a wire is inserted into the base of the flower head, folded over to form a hairpin, then twisted together. This approach is used for several reasons: to use a flower head in an arrangement for which its stem would be too long—such as a boutonniere, halo, wreath, or garland—or to add fragile flowers (such as stephanotis) to a bouquet or arrangement.

a note on numbers

For the sample projects in the Techniques section, you'll find estimates of the numbers of flowers you'll need for specific projects. But as you look through the featured designs, you'll notice the estimates are absent. That's because estimating the size and content of a particular arrangement is not an exact science. Floral design is a very instinctive art—like adding spice to a recipe, you'll find that you add or take away flowers and foliage "to taste." The size of brides varies and so does the size of their bouquets. While a 20-stem rose bouquet might be perfectly proportioned with a bride of average size, it may look big and clunky in the hands of a petite one. Finally, as we mentioned previously, flowers are unpredictable. When the flowers arrive on your wedding day, you may find that you need to substitute out some fading blooms and replace them with whatever you can get your hands on. It's important to stay flexible and improvise if necessary.

Flowers & Essentials

Rose or other flower

Green floral tape

Clippers

22-gauge floral wire

Preparation & Assembly

1. Insert one end of the wire into the base of the flower head, and pull it out on the other side.

2. Twist the end of the wire back onto itself to close the loop, then twist the remaining length of wire down the stem of the flower.

3. Starting at the top, wrap the stem with floral tape.

To Wire a Flower Head without a Stem

1. Cut the flower head from the stem, leaving only about ¼ inch (6 mm) of stem intact.

2. Insert the wire into the base of the head, and pull it out on the other side, twisting the end of the wire back onto itself to close the loop. If you'll be wiring the flower head into a wreath, garland, halo, or other arrangement, you can wrap the remaining length of wire around the form you're using.

3. If you're using the flower head for a boutonniere (see page 42), wrap the remaining length of wire with floral tape. You can also use this technique to wire foliage or to wire the flower head to a stronger piece of wire and insert it in floral foam or a bouquet.

Hand-Tied Bouquet

There are other ways to make a wedding bouquet (such as using wired flowers in a holder), but a hand-tied bouquet is the easiest for the DIY bride, and it's the style favored by most brides and floral designers today. A hand-tied bouquet can look casual or formal and be used to create any of the common bouquet styles (see page 38). This example is a round bouquet, which is an average, medium-sized bouquet. Once you learn this style, you'll be able to make any bouquet style with a few modifications (such as using fewer flowers, a looser arrangement, etc.)

Once you've chosen the flowers for your bouquet, the actual assembly is easy.

Flowers & Essentials

Main flowers (8 to 10)

Accent flowers (6 to 8)

Foliage

Floral supplies (clippers, twine, rubber bands, etc)

4 to 8 pearl-headed corsage pins

3 yards (2.7 cm), 2-inch-wide (5 cm) ribbon

Preparation & Assembly

1. First, condition your flowers (see page 30). Assemble your supplies. Gather the flowers in your hand. Start with the "main" flowers. As you arrange the flowers, try to mix and balance the colors. Fill in any spots between the large flowers with accent flowers or foliage. Keep adding flowers until you have a full compact arrangement that fits com-

fortably in your hand. Add the foliage around the entire bouquet as a "collar." Bind the stems tightly with a piece of twine just below the flower heads, then again with a rubber band about 3 inches (7.6 cm) from the bottom. Recut the stems to even them out and get them to the length you want.

2. Starting about $1^{1}/_{2}$ inches (3.8 cm) from the bottom of the stems, start wrapping the bouquet with a ribbon. Fold the end of the ribbon under itself, then wrap up to the top, covering the twine.

3. Add corsage pins to hold the ribbon in place.

Hand-tied Styles

Your choice of wrapping will have a big effect on the appearance of your finished bouquet. You may wrap the ribbon around the bottom of the stems to cover them up (a more formal look), or leave the bouquet bare-stemmed.

Above: Corsage pins inserted in generous amounts add a decorative effect. The bride's lucky penny is attached to the bouquet with a piece of netting.

Left: The stems of this bouquet are wrapped completely and tied with a bow for a more formal look.

Left: A bare-stemmed bouquet with corsage pins inserted in a neat row creates a formal look that echoes the groom's tuxedo shirt.

bouquet tips

Always make a practice bouquet before your wedding day.

In general, bouquets hold an average of 15 stems, but the number varies greatly depending on the types of flowers used, the style of the bouquet, and even the size of the bride or bridesmaid. Anywhere from one to three dozen stems is normal—one dozen would probably be considered a posy (see page 39), while two dozen or more flowers would be a big bouquet.

Stems are usually cut to 10 to 12 inches (25.4 to 30.5 cm); however, stem size also varies depending on the flower and the style of the bouquet. When cutting the stems, cut a little at a time and test the length in your hand. Once you've got one the right size, use it as a template for cutting the others.

If you'll be transporting the bouquet, keep it in water and cushion the head of the bouquet with tissue paper to protect it. Keep the bouquet soaking in water for as long as possible. When you're ready to use it, remove it from the water and blot the ends with a paper towel so the water doesn't stain your dress.

Kissing Ball

A kissing ball (also known as a flower girl ball or a pomander) is a versatile piece that can be used several ways for a wedding. Traditionally, it was hung from a chandelier over the reception table of the wedding party. That's still a charming use for it, but it can also be hung from chair backs, on pew or aisle ends, over doorknobs, or in doorways. Its most common use, though, is as an alternative bouquet for a flower girl. It hangs over the wrist, leaving her hands free for other duties. Use hardy flowers, but try not to use too many. The ball is shaped with wet floral foam, which becomes weighty, and too many heavy flowers will make it too difficult for a small girl to carry.

Flowers & Essentials

Main flowers (8 to 10)

Accent flowers (6 to 8)

Floral supplies (clippers, scissors, etc.)

Floral foam

Chicken wire

Double-satin ribbon

Preparation & Assembly

1. Cut a piece of floral foam and shape it into a small ball. Soak the ball in a bucket of water (don't run it under a faucet, as this can cause pieces of the foam to break off). The foam is completely soaked when it sinks to the bottom of the bucket. Wrap the ball in chicken wire (this will keep the ball from falling apart, provide additional support for the flowers, and give you somewhere to tie your ribbon).

2. Tie the ribbon through the chicken wire, knotting it underneath and creating a loop handle. Condition your flowers, and cut all the stems to about 2 inches (5 cm) long. Set the ball aright so that you can work on all sides.

3. Begin adding the flowers to the ball, alternating flowers, and varying sizes and colors. Try not to poke more holes than you need, as the ball may start to fall apart. Try to fill all the sides equally so the arrangement still looks round.

bouquet styles

Along with the myriad other decisions you have to make about your bouquet, from the flowers you'll use to the composition of the colors, there are different bouquet shapes to consider. While your choice of flowers may ultimately determine the shape of your bouquet, it's helpful to know the terms florists use to describe different bouquet styles. Thinking about the shape and proportion of your bouquet will help you coordinate it with your dress style. As a general rule, the bigger the dress, the bigger the bouquet. Dress fabrics also play a role—delicate fabrics pair well with delicate flowers; sleek flowers complement highly textured fabrics, such as brocade; and unfussy fabrics like linen or cotton look great with unfussy flowers.

The following guide provides definitions of bouquet styles and suggestions on dress-bouquet combinations.

PRESENTATION BOUQUET

To show off the long slender stems of flowers such as calla lilies, sunflowers, orchids, giant irises, or even roses, many brides opt for a presentation-style bouquet, which is carried in the crook of the arm rather than clutched in both hands. A contemporary bride may even choose to carry a bouquet of long slender branches, such as cherry or apple blossoms or cat-tails, presentation style. This bouquet style complements dresses with straight lines, such as sheaths, slip dresses, and A-line or empire waist dresses.

CASCADE

A cascade bouquet is composed of flowers wired together to spill downward. It's a formal bouquet that generally looks best with formal dress styles, such as the ball gown style.

PHOTO BY WWW.LISAFRECHETTE.COM
FLORAL DESIGN PAUL ECKHART, BROADWAY FLORISTS

POSY

The term posy generally describes a diminutive bouquet of tightly arranged flowers. In Victorian times, the flowers in a posy were arranged in concentric circles, but today the term posy is more loosely applied to any very small bouquet that generally features compact blooms rather than loose or spiky ones. Posies look great with vintage gowns or any dress that's decidedly feminine.

PHOTO BY WWW.ALLEGRASSTUDIO.COM
FLORAL DESIGN SHERRY SPENCER, PAT'S FLORAL DESIGN

NOSEGAY

A nosegay is your basic wedding bouquet, average size, and typically composed of compact flowers rather than loose or spiky ones. It's larger than a posy, so it's versatile, and complements most dress styles, from a ball gown style to a modern sheath.

PHOTO BY WWW.STEPHENSWAIN.COM

KISSING BALL

A kissing ball (also known as a pomander) isn't exactly a bouquet, but rather a type of arrangement that can be carried over the wrist in place of a bouquet, or used as a decoration for chairs, doors, or pews (see page 33). It's often the choice for flower girls.

ROUND

The only difference between a nosegay and a round bouquet is that the flowers in a round bouquet tend to be more loosely arranged. The idea is that the bouquet should be completely three-dimensional, full on all sides. This kind of bouquet can be dramatic, so it's a good choice for a simple dress without a lot of ornamentation.

TUSSY MUSSY

A tussy mussy is a small cone-shaped bouquet holder, usually made of silver or pewter engraved with fanciful flourishes. Victorians composed small bouquets (often intended to convey a message) in tussy mussies and gave them as gifts or carried them to social events or weddings.

Garland

Garlands are great all-purpose decorations for weddings. Use them to decorate the entrance to your ceremony or reception space.

Drape one over a bare mantel or down the stairs you'll descend on your way to the ceremony. Hang one over the top of an arbor to create a beautiful threshold for your ceremony, or from the edges of your reception buffet table. You can even use them to mark off family aisles at the ceremony.

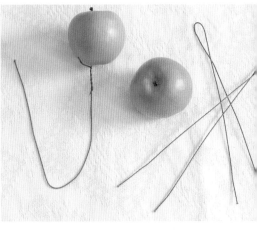

Flowers & Essentials

Branches with leaves (as signature leaves in garland)(about 4)

Green apples or other fruit (4 to 6)

Stephanotis blooms (8 to 12)

Accent leaves (about 6)

22-gauge wire

24-gauge wire

Floral supplies

6 yards (6.4 m) twine

3 yards (2.7 m) 4-inch-wide (10.2 cm) double-satin ribbon

Preparation & Assembly

1. Cut a piece of twine to the length you want for your garland (add a little extra on the end for making a loop from which to tie or hang the garland). Remove the leaves from their branches.

2. Wire the apples by threading a piece of the 22-gauge wire through the bottom and out the other side, twisting the two sides of the wire together at the ends.

3. Gather a handful of signature leaves and accent leaves in your hand, and secure them at the bottom with a piece of wire. Wire stephanotis blossoms (see page 42 for instructions on wiring a flower), and add them to the bunch. Add the wired apple to the bunch. Wire the entire bunch to the twine, leav-

ing a little loose twine at the end for tying.

4. Continue adding bunches of foliage and apples until you have filled almost the length of the twine (leave a little free twine at the end for tying). Loop ribbon through the garland near each end.

Flower Girl Halo

A halo or hair wreath is a sweet accessory for a flower girl, bridesmaid, or even a bride. You can make one with the floral supplies that you have on hand for making other arrangements. This example is as simple as they come, but you can make the design your own by alternating flowers around the halo or tying ribbons or other embellishments to it.

Flowers & Essentials

12 stems tweedia (oxypetalum) or other flower

Heavy-gauge (20 to 22) brown floral wire

24-gauge floral wire

Preparation & Assembly

1. Condition your flowers (see page 30) and keep them soaking in water until ready to use. Create the halo base to fit the flower girl's head. To measure, just fit a piece of wire up to the head to see where it would fit comfortably. Chances are you'll have to use two pieces of wire twisted together to fit. Just overlap the ends and twist until you form a circle of the appropriate size. Start wrapping a piece of 24-gauge floral wire around the circle you created, then tuck a few stems of tweedia under the wire, and wrap it a few times to make sure it's secured to the halo. Don't cut the wire before adding the next bunch—you'll need to use one continuously running piece around the halo.

2. Continue adding bunches of tweedia until you've covered the halo, then cut the wire, and wrap the end back around the halo.

Alternatives

If you use roses, you'll have to wire each flower head individually to the halo for support.

As an alternative headpiece, you may want to hot glue or wire flowers to a hair comb. Use leftover bits of foliage or flowers from your bouquet or table arrangements.

Boutonniere

Boutonnieres add a special soft touch to a serious wedding suit or tux, letting the groom have a little bit of color and texture, too. These instructions are for a single-flower boutonniere, but you can just add foliage or flowers as you like without much more effort.

Flowers & Essentials

Stephanotis bloom or other small bloom

Stephanotis stem

Floral supplies (clippers, floral tape, etc.)

Pearl-tipped corsage pin

Dressmaker's pin

Preparation & Assembly

Stephanotis stems should be kept covered in plastic wrap in a cool, dark place until ready to use. A cooler is a better storage option than a refrigerator because stephanotis can wilt when exposed to the gases emitted by some foods.

1. Soak the stephanotis stem in water. Snap the blossom from its stem.

2. Insert the stephanotis stem through the center of the flower.

3. Wrap the wire base of the stephanotis stem with floral tape. Add a pearl-headed corsage pin in the center of the cotton tip of the stephanotis stem.

To Use

Curl up the taped "stem" of the flower, and tuck it through the buttonhole. Use a dressmaker's pin to attach the boutonniere to the jacket. Start under the lapel, go out, then back under the lapel to fasten it.

Wedding Wreath

Like most wedding traditions, wreaths have symbolism. Just as wedding rings symbolize eternity, the continuous, unbroken circle of the wreath is meant to remind the couple and guests of everlasting love. Wreaths can be used flat on a table with a candle in the center, or hanging from a door, wall, or buffet table. There are several ways to make wreaths, but you may find this is the easiest and most reliable one, which is the kind of method you're looking for on your wedding day.

Flowers & Essentials

24 main blooms

12 bunches of berries or
   other accent blossom

Wire wreath form*

24-gauge floral wire

Floral supplies

3 yards (2.7 m) double-satin,
   4-inch (10.2 cm) wide ribbon

*You can also use a floral foam wreath
 form, or even bend grapevine into the
 shape of a wreath.

Preparation & Assembly

1. Condition your flowers (see page 30) and remove the berries from the branches. After you've allowed the flowers to soak for several hours, recut the stems to about 4 inches (10.2 cm). Start wrapping a spool of wire around the wreath frame. Gather a bunch of flowers and a few berries in your hand and tuck them under the back of the frame. Wrap the wire around the stems several times to secure them in place. Don't cut the

wire—you'll need to use one piece of wire continuously around the frame.

2. Keep adding bunches of flowers and berries around the wreath until it's full. Wrap the wire several times around the final bunch of flowers and berries, then cut it, and wrap the end around the frame.

3. Cut the ribbon to the length you want, then tie the cut ends around the frame in the top center of the wreath, creating a loop from which you will hang the wreath.

Table & Site Arrangements

While you may never have put together a handheld bouquet before, chances are you've made a table arrangement at some point for a dinner party or just to enjoy in your home. Making a wedding table arrangement is no more difficult, but of course there are some special considerations.

First of all, the table arrangements need to look comfortable in your reception space. Keep proportion (that all-important design consideration) in mind as you start to plan your designs. A tiny centerpiece might look unimpressive in an open, airy hall with tall ceilings, and a tall glass vase filled with long-stemmed blooms might look cramped in a cozy room. Consider the shape of your tables (round, rectangular, or square) and the interaction of your guests. You don't want them to have to strain their necks to carry on a conversation around a large centerpiece. Try to make your arrangement look good from all angles at which it will be seen. If it will be backed by a wall on one side, it doesn't need to be round (meaning you can use fewer flowers for the back), but you should try to create the impression that it looks the same all around. You can do this by leaning the flowers back, up, and out to the sides.

SHAPES

In general, arrangements can be described as having one of several shapes: curved, triangular, conical, rectangular, or low and compact.

Curved

Creates a rounded, fan shape coming from the container. Can be used for a front-facing or all-around display.

Triangular

Can be created with a low, wide-mouthed vase and floral foam or frogs to hold flowers up in the middle.

Conical

This style is created by a narrow-mouthed container and flowers or foliage with some height.

Low and Compact

Created with a low, round container, should be filled out in all sides

Rectangular

This is useful with flowers that have some height.

CONTAINERS

The right container is also key to a successful arrangement. Matching flowers and containers above all requires experimentation and patience. You may try the same flowers in several different containers before getting it right, or need to add or remove flowers for just the right balance. Keep in mind, though, that you should choose the container to fit the flower, and not vice versa. As

Left: Look for pieces that originally served another purpose, such as these creamware serving pieces. They're unexpected and interesting. Middle: Antique silver service pieces filled with loose, charming flowers create an atmosphere of genteel hospitality. Right: For table arrangements, white is always right. Mismatched pieces of milkglass collected from yard sales or flea markets look great with almost anything from informal garden flowers to roses.

you play with your arrangements, looking for the perfect fit, keep the following considerations in mind.

Shape of Container

First, consider the mouth of the vase. Is it wide or narrow, square, rectangular, round, or cylindrical?

For beginners, it's easier to use a cylindrical or narrow-mouthed container, which keeps flowers in place naturally. A trumpet-shaped container is also easy to use. It keeps flowers in place at the base, then lets them spread out at the top. If you use a wide-mouthed container, your flowers will spread out naturally unless you use a support, such as a frog or wet floral foam, to hold them in place or create a grid across the mouth of the vase with floral tape. If you're using a clear glass container, you'll have to think of

a way to hide your support method, such as covering it with moss or another type of filler.

Formal or Informal

Aside from the shape, the material your container is made of will affect the look. From galvanized steel buckets to terra-cotta pots to woven baskets or clear glass, you've got a lot of choices. Pick materials that harmonize or contrast with your flowers. For example, wildflowers in a maple syrup bucket say rustic country wedding, but in a mint julep cup, they're a little more formal.

Adapting Containers

If you've got an interesting opaque container, such as a gourd, but it's not watertight, you can hide an inexpensive (and even unsightly) watertight container inside it. Drinking glasses, plastic bowls, or water pitchers can all be pressed into service for this purpose. You can also line the container with a heavy-duty piece of plastic (such as a piece of a lawn and leaf bag), securing it to the sides of the container with heavy tape or staples to keep it from leaking.

If the container you want to use is too deep for your flowers, you can insert some sort of block in the bottom, then put a piece of floral foam on top of it to raise the flowers up.

If you find a basket or other container with the right shape but the wrong appearance, transform it by hot gluing real or silk leaves (or even pieces of bamboo) to its surface, or cover the container with a beautiful piece of fabric, then tie it with ribbon or raffia.

Hollow out fruits or vegetables, such as artichokes, red peppers, or apples, and insert a watertight container in the center for a distinctive container.

Adapting Flowers

You can also adapt a flower to fit a certain container. If you find out that your stems are too short, you can add length by wiring them (see page 32), essentially creating a fake, longer stem.

SAMPLE TABLE ARRANGEMENTS

The best way to achieve the look you're going for is to experiment with different flowers and containers (see page 46 for ideas). The examples provided here cover a range of seasons and levels of formality. Use them as inspiration, substituting flowers and containers to fit the look of your wedding.

Semi-Formal Wedding, Any Season

At a round table (above), a low, round bowl creates an appealing symmetry. This arrangement breaks with tradition by placing several individual flower heads in small, separate bowls within a larger one. Petals scattered all over the table seem to spread a festive feeling. It's an informal look, but the choice of roses gives it a touch of elegance.

PHOTO BY WWW.ROBERTMARCOS.COM
FLORAL DESIGN STACIE BARBA, DAY OF ELEGANCE

PHOTO BY WWW.OPPENHEIMPHOTO.COM

Left: A humble paint bucket doesn't have to look rustic: paired with a low cluster of (silk) hydrangeas, it's elegant. Right: A simple white basket filled with delicate flowers is a delightful and affordable centerpiece.

FLORAL DESIGNS WWW.BLOOM-ROOM.COM

Semi-Formal to Formal
Summer Wedding
(conical)

The tall, sleek stems of allium giantum (available summer through fall) are showcased in a tall glass vase (above), which supports their stems and doesn't distract attention from their simple beauty.

Since the table arrangement is so spare, the place settings are given a little extra interest by a single dendrobium orchid bloom and a sprig of green viburnum berries.

Compact Semi-Formal
Fall Arrangement
(curved)

This arrangement (above, center) says semi-formal fall wedding, but what exactly is it that brings the look together?

The saturated colors of the flowers are in harmony with the colors of the table linens and dinner plates. Burgundy dahlias, orange zinnias, and chocolate cymbidium orchids are the feature flowers that anchor the arrangement in the center. They are in a tight, rather than loose, arrangement, which adds a feeling of formality (even though dahlias and zinnias aren't considered to be formal flowers). Chocolate cosmos pods are placed at a slightly higher level than the flowers to give texture and prevent the arrangement from looking too uniform. Viburnum berries and leaves fill in and give a little texture and contrast. The compact black vase pulls everything together and adds sophistication.

Semi-Formal Spring
Cluster Arrangement
(triangular)

This cluster of flowers in a silver tea service (above, right) brings to mind a charming garden wedding. How is this look achieved? The different pieces in the service are of varying heights and shapes, so the bouquet in each varies. The large center arrangement is full and lush. Hyacinths, lady's mantle, and a few spikes of delphinium add color and fullness. The white hydrangea and Vendela roses anchor the arrangement at the base. The two smaller silver pieces bring the attention down to the containers. The sugar service is filled with a single, bushy stem of white hydrangea, while the tiny creamer is filled with delicate lamb's ear and rosemary. The arrangement forms a triangle, which naturally draws the eye from the top down to the outside edges.

let them eat flowers

EDIBLE FLOWERS

Calendula

Pansy

Marigold

Lavender

Violet

Nasturtium

POISONOUS OR TOXIC FLOWERS

Anemone

Azalea

Buttercup

Calla lily

Daffodil

Delphinium

Foxglove

Hyacinth

Hydrangea

Lily of the valley

Lupine

Mistletoe

Monk's hood

Queen Anne's lace

Sweet pea

Note: This list includes only some popular wedding flowers. Always investigate the flower before putting it onto your cake.

Cake Toppers

Your cake may be unadorned or covered in sugar or icing flowers, which is perfectly lovely. But if you're looking for a charming embellishment, you may suggest that your cake baker use real flowers.

Cake flowers may be as simple as a single bloom atop the uppermost layer of a cake, or a handful of petals sprinkled around the plate. On the other end of the spectrum are arrangements built in floral foam and placed in between layers of the cake. If a friend or family member is making your cake, you'll probably want to avoid elaborate cakes with columns and layers of support built in anyway, so there's no need to worry about working flowers into an architectural marvel.

If you decide to use real flowers, the easiest way to go is to use leftover blooms or petals from the flowers used for the bouquets or table arrangements. It will save you the trouble of having to order extra flowers, and will help tie the cake to the rest of your wedding theme. There is a caveat, though. You'll need to make sure your flowers have not been treated with chemicals or pesticides, and that they are not poisonous flowers that could leave a dangerous residue on the cake. If you're not sure whether or not your flowers are organic and chemical free, it's best to err on the safe side. Although the liklihood of a guest getting sick from a small trace amount of chemicals rubbing off on cake icing are very slim, why take a chance?

Some safe flowers to consider are orchids, tulips, gardenias, daisies, and of course roses. These flowers are inherently non-toxic, but again, you'll need to find out if your flowers in particular have been sprayed with chemicals.

If you're using flowers from your garden, wash the blooms and let them dry on a paper towel. Put them in plastic bags and freeze them until just before you are going to put them on the cake.

One trick to keeping flowers fresh on a cake is to cut a 3-inch (7.6 cm) piece from a drinking straw and tape it closed on one end. Fill the straw with water and stick the flowers in it, like a mini vase. You can then poke the closed end of the straw into the top of the cake.

Some other options are to use crystallized edible flowers (coated in egg white and superfine sugar), such as pansies and violets, or use silk flowers.

The Party's Over

Make It Last

Marriage is about forever and eternity; flowers are by nature temporary. Long after your wedding day is over, you can still remember the beauty of your flowers and bouquet if you preserve them. There are several ways to go about doing this. The method you choose depends on the hardiness and shape of the flower.

Pressing

For flowers with flat, delicate petals, such as sweet peas and cosmos, try using a flower press or just pressing between sheets of acid-free paper under a heavy object like a book.

Hanging Upside Down

Many flowers (especially hardier ones, such as roses) will retain their shape if hung upside down to dry. Choose a cool dark place, like a basement, preferably a place where there's some ventilation. First remove any leaves, which could attract bugs. Take apart the bouquet and hang flowers individually or in small bunches from a piece of twine. Make sure that individual flower heads don't touch each other. That can damage the petals and cause the dried flower to crumble. The flowers should dry within three weeks.

In the Vase

If your table arrangements (or bouquets) consist mainly of wildflowers, you can try them standing up in a vase filled with a little water. Place the vase in a cool, dark place and the flowers should dry after about a week.

Freeze-Dried Flowers

For practically foolproof preservation (at a cost), you can have your flowers professionally freeze-dried. The process will preserve your flowers in their exact shape and position. Freeze-drying also helps preserve the flowers' color almost exactly—an obvious advantage over hang drying. Freeze-drying is done by big, expensive, high-tech machines, so it's a process that can't be duplicated at home. If you do decide to try freeze-drying, have it done as soon as possible after the wedding, while your flowers are still in good shape. This means that if you're leaving right away for your honeymoon, you should delegate the responsibility to a helper.

PHOTO BY WWW.ANREMAIER.COM

checklist for the big day

It's easy for things to slip through the cracks when you're juggling the many details involved in planning a wedding. To help you keep track of your flower plans, here's a list of tasks and a timetable for completing them.

DAY BEFORE CEREMONY

Pick up flowers or have them delivered

Condition flowers and leave soaking in water in a cool dark place or cooler (unless otherwise instructed)

Make sure you have all needed supplies: clippers, twine, rubber bands, floral tape, floral wire, floral foam (if necessary), embellishments, containers

DAY OF CEREMONY

Recut stems if necessary before arranging

Mist flowers with water if the wedding is not until late afternoon or evening

Assign helper for distribution of bouquets and boutonnieres

Assign helper for setup and breakdown of ceremony and reception arrangements

Dry bouquet stems after removing from water so they don't stain your dress

Monochromatic Palette

One of the hottest trends in wedding flowers today, monochromatic bouquets and arrangements are not only stylish, they're a foolproof solution for a DIY bride. A monochromatic scheme keeps it simple—once you've chosen a color, stay loosely within that range for all your flowers. While your color may be consistent, play around with texture—a creamy rose next to a spiky dahlia—and composition—a bouquet featuring a single type of flower, or a melange of compact flowers paired with loose, frilly foliage.

The following section of the book explores five different color palettes: pink, white, red, orange/yellow, and blue. Whether your style is traditional or modern, you'll be inspired by how versatile a monochromatic palette can be.

Pretty in Pink

E ven if you've never considered yourself a big fan of pink, take another look before dismissing it from your flower plan. It's one of the most versatile color palettes for wedding flowers. From dainty pastels to shocking fuchsia or cerise, pinks make an impression.

Soft romantic flowers with delicate textures such as peonies or sweet peas are one way to go. If you're looking for drama, consider the bold, graphic dahlia, or the gerbera daisy, both of which come in several shades of pink. Fresh cherry blossoms, delicate dendrobium orchids, blushing pink winterberries, and elegant tulips can go either way, looking sophisticated or simply sweet.

Very Important Pinks

SPRING
Azalea
Cherry blossom
Peony
Tulip
Dogwood
Flowering quince
Mimosa

SUMMER
Asiatic lily
Astilbe
Bougainvillea
Cosmos
Gerbera daisy
Rose
Pinks (dianthus)
Queen of the prairie
Rhododendron
Sweet pea
Stargazer lily

FALL
Allium
Aster
Chrysanthemum
Dahlia
Zinnia

WINTER
Camellia
Heather
Hellebore
Iceland poppy
Poinsettia

Think Pink Gerberas

Gerbera daisies are all about understated elegance and unabashed joy. The gerbera positively radiates cheerfulness and optimism—what more could you ask for from a wedding flower?

Gerberas are bold enough to stand on their own without other flowers or foliage, and hardy enough to withstand a hot day in a bride's hands. The gerbera's simple shape has a modern, graphic quality that feels equally at home at a chic urban wedding or a homey backyard affair. Here are three designs (a bouquet, a boutonniere, and a table arrangement) that feature gerberas in different shades of pink.

If you love the flower, but you're not convinced about the pink, gerberas also come in an amazing variety of colors: white, orange, salmon, scarlet, burgundy, or yellow. Each has a distinctive yet just as cheery feel. There are single and semi-double petal varieties and mini-gerberas, too.

flower facts

Botanical Name
Gerbera Jamesonii

Other Names
Gerbera, African daisy, Transvaal daisy, Barberton daisy

Bloom Time
Summer to fall

Availability
Can be ordered most of the year; relatively inexpensive, but shipping cost can be high (gerberas are shipped in special trays to keep their stems upright)

Hardiness
Long-lasting and hardy

Bride and bridesmaids carry different hues of pink: bold for the bride, muted for the maid of honor, and a softer shade for the bridesmaids.

Boutonniere

A single hot pink gerbera paired with a galax leaf and a stem of wax weed adds a touch of color and fun to an otherwise serious suit.

Hand-tied posy

Flowers & Essentials

Dark pink gerberas (Serena)

Medium-pink gerberas (Rosula)

Light pink gerberas (Rozamunde)

Floral supplies

Ribbon

Preparation & Assembly

1. Condition for flowers with soft stems (see page 31). There are no leaves on gerberas, so there's no foliage to remove. After cutting, let the stems soak in deep water for as long as possible.

2. Arrange the flowers in the hand tightly to form a posy, then bind, wrap, and pin (see page 34).

3. Since the stems are flexible and tend to bend, carefully wrap brown paper around the whole bouquet (including the heads), and keep it in an upright container until just before the ceremony or photos.

Table arrangement

Flowers & Essentials

Gerbera daisies

*Square dinner plate or
    other square dish*

Floral supplies

Wet floral foam

Chicken wire (optional)

Preparation & Assembly

1. Condition the flowers according to the instructions for soft stems (see page 31).

2. Cut a piece of floral foam to fit in the dish you'll be using. You may need to cut it in half heightwise to make sure the arrangement is flat and close to the plate. Soak the foam in a bucket or bowl of water until it sinks (at that point it's got enough water in it to feed the flowers). Wrap the wet foam in chicken wire (optional).

3. Cut the stems at a diagonal about 2 inches (5 cm) below the flower head. Insert the flowers into the foam close enough together that you can't see the foam. This arrangement should stay fresh for three days.

This arrangement is ideal for rectangular tables or a long banquet table, especially one with overhead lighting. A shallow but not completely flat square plate serves as a container. No water is necessary—the flowers are inserted into a wet square of floral foam, which feeds them water throughout the day.

Heavenly Heather Bouquet

The hardy heather is no wallflower—it's bold, romantic, and can hold its own without any foliage or additional flowers. This bright pink variety looks brilliant against a pure white dress, but there are dozens of varieties of heather available, in shades ranging from white to yellow to bright red. If you don't want a whole bouquet, consider using it as an accent plant. It's a versatile bloom with a lot of potential.

PHOTO BY WWW.LISAFRECHETTE.COM FLORAL DESIGN JOLLI HOWLETT, BOTANICA FLOWERS

Hand-tied round bouquet

Flowers & Essentials
Pink heather
Floral supplies
Ribbon

Preparation & Assembly

1. Condition the stems following the procedure for woody stems (see page 30). Pick out any dead or loose flowers.

2. This bouquet should be assembled in the hand so that it's well rounded and equally full on each side. Assemble a small bunch in the hand first, bind it (see page 34), then tie it with a generous amount of ribbon, leaving the ends free (no bows). Surround the small bouquet with more stems, again making sure it doesn't look lopsided.

3. Bind and tie it again, then finish with white ribbon and corsage pins.

flower facts

Botanical Name
Erica vulgaris, Calluna vulgaris

Bloom Time
November to April

Availability
Easiest to find in autumn through spring, but can be imported other times of the year. Moderately priced.

Hardiness
Hardy, but care should be taken not to handle the flower stems too much, as individual flowers on the stem may loosen.

Pink Roses, Plus

Pink roses are feminine and romantic—a classic choice for wedding bouquets and arrangements. But the following three arrangements show how versatile a palette of pink roses can be. From a contemporary pink bouquet to a charming kissing ball and a touching heart-shaped wreath, these pink rose arrangements are anything but ordinary.

Hand-tied nosegay

Flowers & Essentials

Candy Bianca roses

Pink cymbidium orchids

White hyacinth florets

Floral supplies

Ribbon

Corsage pins

Preparation & Assembly

1. Cut the orchids from their stems and create wire stems for them (see page 32). Cut the florets (flower heads) from the stem of the hyacinth and wire them.

2. If you want, wire the roses for further support of their stems.

3. Combine a few stems in your hand, and continue adding stems, mixing textures.

4. Bind and wrap the bouquet (see page 34) with ribbon. Add pearl-headed corsage pins.

flower facts

Availability

All the flowers in the bouquet can be ordered year-round

Hardiness

Roses will last for several days; orchids and hyacinths need to be kept in water whenever possible

A word on roses

Roses are flowering shrubs, so they should be conditioned the same way as other woody-stemmed flowers (see page 30). The added work for roses is removing the thorns. Make sure you're wearing gloves when you handle roses. Use a sharp knife to cut off the thorns, and remove all additional foliage.

Kissing ball

Flowers & Essentials

Soft pink spray roses

Medium-pink spray roses

Magenta spray roses

Floral supplies

Floral foam

Chicken wire

Ribbon

Preparation & Assembly

1. Cut the spray roses from their stems, leaving the stems about 3 inches (7.6 cm) long.

2. Follow the instructions for creating a kissing ball on page 37. Try to create evenly distributed clusters of color by placing three to five roses of one color next to each other.

3. If it's a hot day, mist the kissing ball frequently to keep the petals from browning.

Heart-shaped wreath

Flowers & Essentials

Pink sweetheart roses

Floral supplies

Heart-shaped floral foam wreath

Hot glue gun and glue sticks

Ribbon

Preparation & Assembly

1. When choosing roses for the wreath, try to find blooms that have just started to open. Condition roses according to the instructions on page 30. Cut each stem just below the flower head.

2. Tie the ribbon at the top of the wreath form, forming a loop from which to hang the wreath. You'll want the ribbon to be very secure, as the wreath will become heavy.

3. Begin hot gluing the flower heads to the form at the outer edges of the wreath. Make sure you place the flower heads as close together as possible. Keep filling in additional rows of roses until you reach the center of the wreath. You may need to fill in gaps with tightly closed buds.

PHOTO BY WWW.ROBERTMARCOS.COM   FLORAL DESIGN STACIE BARBA, DAY OF ELEGANCE

White Wedding

Not too long ago most brides wouldn't have even considered carrying a wedding bouquet that was anything but white. With all the options available today, white remains a popular choice for wedding flowers because of all the gorgeous white blooms available year-round. But while white may be a traditional choice of color, you still have lots of room to play around with interesting shapes, textures, and arrangements.

From formal white roses to freewheeling daisies, delicate stephanotis to die-hard dahlias, you can find white flowers that fit the mood and feel of your wedding. White calla lilies are exquisitely simple and fit right in at a formal wedding or a more casual affair. White tulips, too, are versatile; modern or traditional, formal or informal—they'll shine in any setting. Remember, too, that there's not just a single shade of white: oyster, pearl, ivory, and cream are just a few variations on pure white. It's important to keep this in mind when choosing the flower, since it may clash with the shade in your dress (bring a swatch of your dress fabric with you when choosing flowers).

Wonderful Whites

SPRING

Anemone coronair ("the bride")
Azalea (rhododendron)
Easter lily
Freesia
Iris
Lilac
Lily of the valley
Magnolia
Narcissus (narcissus, daffodil)
Ranunculus
Tulip

SUMMER

Cosmos
Daisy
Gardenia
Ginger lily
Honeysuckle
Mexican orange blossom

FALL

Aster
Chrysanthemum
Dahlia
Tuberose

WINTER

Camellia
Christmas rose
Snowdrops
Snowberry
Poinsettia
Mistletoe
White forsythia

YEAR-ROUND

Calla lily
Casablanca lily
Moth orchid
Rose
Stephanotis

Lovely Lily of the Valley Bouquet

The impossibly delicate lily of the valley is nothing if not romantic. Its tiny, bell-shaped flowers and intoxicating fragrance have made it one of the new favorites in wedding flowers. All that beauty does come at a price: lily of the valley is one of the more expensive cut flowers available. The good news is that you need only a few stems and no additional foliage for a gorgeous bouquet—the simpler the better. This is an easy bouquet to make and should last well through the day if kept in water as long as possible.

PHOTO BY WWW.ELOISEFARR.COM   FLORAL DESIGN MARCY MOERMAN

Hand-tied posy

Flowers & Essentials

Lily of the valley

Floral supplies

Ribbon

Preparation & Assembly

1. Condition the flowers according to the instructions for soft stems (see page 31). When you're ready to make the bouquet, recut the stems under warm water.

2. Assemble the stems by hand, and bind and wrap as you would for any hand-tied bouquet (see page 34).

3. Keep the bouquet in water up until the last minute, then make sure to dry the stems to avoid dripping water on dresses.

flower facts

Botanical Name

Convallaria magalis

Bloom Time

Early spring

Availability

Can be ordered until late spring; expensive

Hardiness

Very fragile; will need to be kept in water as long as possible; avoid touching

fragrant white flowers & herbs

Asiatic lily

Casablanca lily

Eucalyptus

Frangipani

Freesia

Gardenia

Heliotrope

Honeysuckle

Lavender

Lilac

Lily of the valley

Jasmine

Mint

Mexican orange blossom

Mock orange

Paperwhite

Peonies

Rose (Double Delight, David Austin, Prospero, Golden Celebration [to name a few])

Rosemary

Sweet bay magnolia

Sweet pea

Stephanotis

Tuberose

White ginger

PHOTO BY WWW.UNRUEPHOTO.COM

The gardenia's scent is intoxicating and its creamy, rich leaves and waxy petals are a visual treat. A gardenia's beauty is short lived though, so use them carefully in your wedding flower plan. They're perfect as a single flower in the hair.

Calla Lily Bouquet

The key words for this bouquet are simple and elegant. The calla lily's strong, slender stems distinguish it as one of the most graceful of flowers. Like any good feature, the callas' stems should be shown off, not hidden, so it's best to leave them bare-stemmed rather than wrap up the ends. This bouquet is carried presentation style, in the crook of the arm, again to show off the flower's beautiful form and complement the lines of a straight sheath or ballgown–style wedding or bridesmaid dress. Calla lilies aren't cheap, but don't let that discourage you. A small clutch of a few callas looks even better than a large bouquet of them.

Hand-tied presentation bouquet

Flowers & Essentials
White calla lilies

Bear grass (dasylirion)

Green tye leaves

Floral supplies

Ribbon

Preparation & Assembly

1. This bouquet is easy to make, so it can be made at the very last minute to ensure the freshness of the flowers. Condition the flowers according to the instructions for hollow-stemmed flowers (see page 31).

2. Place a small bunch of the grass and leaves on a table. Lay one of the flowers on top of them with the point facing up. Position the other stems to the side so that the arrangement forms an arrow shape.

3. When you're happy with the shape, tie it with a rubber band. Add French wired ribbon (tied in a bow) over the rubber band to hide the mechanics. Trim the stems to the size you want.

Calla lilies are somewhat delicate and will bruise easily when touched, so avoid touching the flower head. They will last out of water for several hours, but try to submerge the bouquet in water when you're not carrying it.

This darling flower girl posy is composed of mini-calla lilies, stephanotis, and cream roses. Each flower has a slightly different shade and texture, contributing to a delicate overall effect. Tiny stephanotis florets are wired into an ivy halo in her hair (see page 41 for wiring instructions).

flower facts

Botanical Name
Zantedeschia

Bloom Time
Summer

Availability
Available year-round; expensive

Hardiness
Will start to wilt when removed from water, so keep bouquets hydrated as long as possible

PHOTO BY WWW.BARBERPHOTOGRAPHY.COM

Sweet Stephanotis Bouquet

In the Victorian language of flowers (see box, right), stephanotis means "wedded bliss." No wonder this petite star-shaped white flower, nicknamed "the wedding flower" is among the flowers most requested by brides for their bouquets. Stephanotis flowers are delicate and intensely fragrant with firm, waxy petals. They grow on a vine, and their stems are so fragile that the flowers have to be removed from the stem and placed on an artificial stem (there are ones made especially for stephanotis). A small all-stephanotis bouquet allows each stem to shine, but this flower is also great as an accent flower in a mixed bouquet.

Before you fall under the spell of this enchanting little flower, though, consider some practicalities. Stephanotis bruises and fades quickly out of water, so unless you're extremely careful, you may end up with a brown bouquet instead of a white one. Wiring each stem individually is time consuming, so this is not an easy bouquet to make yourself, and it's an expensive one to have made. If you're undeterred by these little drawbacks, a stephanotis bouquet can be an exquisite accessory on your wedding day.

Hand-tied stephanotis posy

Flowers & Essentials

Stephanotis
  (about three dozen blooms)

Stephanotis stems

Pearled corsage pins

Ribbon

Gardenia leaves

Floral supplies

flower facts

Botanical Name
Stephanotis floribunda

Other Names
Wedding flower, Madagascar jasmine, Bride's flower

Bloom Time
Spring to early fall

Availability
Year-round; expensive

Hardiness
Very fragile (about a 3-day life span)

Preparation & Assembly

1. Rather than dunking the delicate stems in water (you should avoid getting water directly on the flower), insert them in a piece of wet floral foam until you're ready to work. Insert the flowers and wet foam in a plastic bag to protect the blooms.

Stephanotis flowers need to be kept chilled as long as possible before use. Don't put them in the refrigerator with foods, though—they'll wilt easily when exposed to gases from certain foods. Place them in a separate cooler with ice until you're ready to prepare the bouquet.

2. You'll need one stephanotis stem per bloom. The tip of the stem is a tube-shaped piece of cotton designed to absorb water and keep the flower hydrated (see picture on page 22). Soak each "fake" stem in water. Snap the blossom off the real stem, then insert the fake stephanotis stem through the center of the bloom.

3. Insert a pearl-headed corsage pin in the cotton tip of the stem (it will look like there is a pearl at the center of the flower). Wrap each stem with floral tape.

4. Gather the stems together, and wrap them with floral tape. Add foliage, and wrap again with floral tape. Wrap with ribbon, and pin with pearl-headed corsage pins.

the victorian language of flowers

Because of strict codes of conduct and prim morality, the Victorians remained discreet in revealing their sentiments by expressing them through the language of flowers, or *florigraphy*. This highly refined language of flowers, originally from the harems of Turkey, so flourished in Europe that books existed to clarify its rules of grammar, and dictionaries sprang up to explain each flower's interpretation. The first such dictionary, *Le Langage des Fleurs*, published in Paris in 1818, had 18 subsequent editions.

One could "utter" whole sentences by combining colors and varieties with plants and herbs, while varying position and foliage. Leaves left on the stem indicated the affirmative; conversely, removing foliage negated the floral meaning.

Messages could be formulated on greeting cards with illustrated blooms, or in small bouquets known as tussy mussies or nosegays. Both men and women wore tussy mussies, which served as tokens of love, simple friendship, or familial bonds. Florigraphy conveyed not only love and happiness, however; a well-chosen flower could express coquetry, dalliance, indifference, or coolness, or it might ridicule, rebuff, refuse, scorn, or insult.

The tradition of florigraphy actually dates back to much earlier times than the Victorian era. The ancient Greeks associated flowers with symbolism derived from classical legends such as the tales of Narcissus and Hyacinth, and some Elizabethan poetry described floral meanings. The Victorian popularity of florigraphy contributed to an increase in letter writing, which in turn has been credited with the establishment of the postal service. Furthermore, the Victorians had a great enthusiasm for gardening, and during the 19th century, flowers were considered more suitable than jewelry for young ladies to wear.

Although many books appeared on the subject of florigraphy, few consistently applied the same meanings and rules. If you're interested, you may wish to apply some floral meanings to your wedding day flowers.

Simply Red

PHOTO BY WWW.UNRUEPHOTO.COM   FLORAL DESIGN ANN MARTIN, EUROPEAN FLORAL

Radiant Red Flowers

SPRING
Anemone
Azalea
English daisy
Freesia
Peony
Tulip

SUMMER
Asiatic lily
Cockscomb
Gerbera daisy
Hibiscus
Rose
Snapdragon
Stock

FALL
Aster
Chrysanthemum
Dahlia
Zinnia

WINTER
Amaryllis
Camellia
Poinsettia
Winterberry

YEAR-ROUND
Calla lily
Rose

Red is the color of love, passion, and intensity. In Chinese tradition, it's the color of good fortune. In terms of symbolism, you can't get a much more potent color than red for your wedding flowers. Red on red is a striking palette. There are so many reds, from the deep, velvety red of Black Magic roses, to the vibrant red of the Zorro dahlia. Depending on your choice of flowers, a red arrangement can be traditional and romantic or contemporary or dramatic. Contrast red flowers with dark green foliage or blue accent flowers for a rich, saturated look. Red flowers on a white or green background pop with color. Try mixing textures for interest—a delicate spray of azalea blossoms can share a vase with hardy roses, and a papery peony can sit comfortably in a bouquet next to a cheerful English daisy. The rose family alone offers dozens of types of red with variations in color and texture.

Rhapsody in Red

This is a monochromatic palette at its best. Subtle variations of color and unexpected combinations of texture make the two designs (a bouquet on the facing page and a flower girl halo below) modern and appealing. The dresses, flowers, and ribbon are well matched and complementary without being too "matchy"—a sophisticated result for a contemporary bride or bridesmaid.

flower facts

Availability
Late summer flowers and year-round flowers; moderately priced in season

Hardiness
All the flowers in the bouquet can last up to seven days with proper conditioning

Flower girl halo

This darling flower girl halo is made from the same spray roses used for the bridesmaids' bouquets. Each rose is wired (see page 32), then wired to the halo in a compact arrangement. The deep red blooms are placed randomly through clusters of pink ones for interest and texture.

Hand-tied posy

Flowers & Essentials

*Cherry red and hot pink
    spray roses*

*Cherry red and hot pink
    mini dahlias*

Floral supplies

Ribbon

Floral preservative spray

Preparation & Assembly

1. Condition for soft stems and roses
(see page 31). Leave flowers to drink
overnight in an upright vase in a cool,
dark place.

2. Arrange the flowers in the hand,
and bind (see page 34), then recut
stems to appropriate length. Let the
bouquet sit in an upright vase (with
just enough water for the flowers to
drink), and spray with a preservative
spray. Once the preservative has
dried, wipe the water from the stems
and wrap with ribbon.

*Roses, tulips, gerbera daisies, and
    mums in different shades of red
    make a rich, textural bouquet.*

Roses are Red

Red roses and romance are so inextricably linked that they may be the first flower you think of when you start your wedding flower planning. Even though a rose may seem a straightforward choice, there are hundreds of varieties of roses (and dozens of red ones), so you've still got a lot of decisions to make—dark burgundy, crimson, or scarlet? Single flowered or double flowered? Tea or English rose? Then there's the whole question of whether to go for an all-rose bouquet or add some other flowers or foliage for texture. Here are some examples you may want to emulate.

PHOTO BY WWW.PHOTOGRAPHER.COM

Hand-tied round bouquet

Flowers & Essentials
Red roses
Floral supplies
Ribbon

Preparation & Assembly

1. Condition the roses for woody stems (see page 30).

2. To get the round shape of this bouquet, start with a single rose. Surround the first flower with concentric circles of roses, holding them tightly as you go.

3. When you've got the shape you want, bind the bouquet tightly. Braid the ribbon up the stem, just as you would your hair.

flower facts

Botanical Name
Rosa

Bloom Time
Varies; generally late spring to fall, some fall rebloom

Availability
Year-round; moderately priced to expensive

Hardiness
Varies by type; generally hardy, lasts up to seven days as a cut flower; can withstand a day out of water, but should be kept out of direct heat

rose varieties

Black Beauty (deep burgundy, black-tipped petals)

Black Magic (deep scarlet)

Charlotte (crimson, double flower)

Don Juan (large, double flower, fragrant)

Dynamite (large flower, ruffled petals)

Love (crimson flowers that are white on the back)

Romeo (deep scarlet, velvety texture, double flower)

Scarlet Knight (deep crimson flowers with tea scent)

Sacha (deep scarlet, urn-shaped flower)

Wedding Day Blues

PHOTO BY WWW.BARBERPHOTOGRAPHY.COM

Why not choose the rarest of flowers for the most special of days? While a profusion of flowers in reds, yellows, and pinks inhabits the common garden and flower shop, deep blue and violet blooms are harder to come by, making them that much more special. Some flower enthusiasts even insist there's no such thing as a blue flower—only varying shades of purple—while others point to delphinium or Himalayan poppies as true blues. Whichever camp you fall into, consider a palette of dreamy violets, delicate lilacs, or blackish blues for your wedding flowers.

Blue and purple flowers tend to be delicate, so you may want to add them to mixed bouquets and arrangements as accents. Combine blues and purples with whites, greens, reds, and pinks to create harmony, or mix them with yellows and oranges for a sharp contrast.

Brilliant Blues

SPRING
Anemone
Bachelor's buttons
  (centaurea)
Blue star (amsonia)
Corydalis
Forget-me-not (myosotis)
Grape hyacinth (muscari)
Hyacinth
Iris
Lilac
Pansy
Violet

SUMMER
Bellflower (campanula)
Cranesbill geranium
Delphinium
Himalayan blue poppy
  (meconopis grandis)
Hydrangea
Leadwort (plumbago)
Love-in–a-mist (nigella)
Lupine
Pincushion flower
  (scabiosa)
Salvia
Texas bluebonnet
Veronica

FALL
Aster
Dephinium (rebloom)
Globe thistle
Gentian
Monkshood

WINTER
African violet
Hellebore
Poppy anemone

YEAR-ROUND
Tweedia (oxypetalum)

BLUE FOLIAGE
Blue cedar
Blue cypress
Ice blue juniper

This dreamy bouquet in blues and purples features fuchsia dendrobium orchid, lavender stock, purple lisianthus, lavender hydrangea, purple statice, and nandina foliage.

Sky Blue Hydrangeas

Delicate and voluptuous, blue hydrangeas are a captivating choice for wedding flowers. The frothy blooms seem to float in the hands of a bride or bridesmaid. They need no additional flowers or foliage for support—a dozen or so blooms make a full, showy bouquet that's simple but chic. Or, combine them with a few other country-garden favorites for casual table arrangements.

flower facts

Bloom Time
Summer

Availability
Available late spring through fall; relatively expensive

Hardiness
Will last as a cut flower for four to six days; can be hung upside down or left in a vase to dry

Table arrangement in mason jar

Flowers & Essentials
Blue hydrangea
Gooseneck loosestrife
Queen Anne's lace
Lavender mums
Floral supplies

Preparation & Assembly

1. When picking garden hydrangeas, pick older blooms—they work best if the flowers are going to be out of water for some time. Older blooms are identified as those that have dried slightly on the bush.

Condition the hydrangeas for woody stems (see page 30). Condition the Queen Anne's lace for hollow stems (see page 31).

2. Arrange the flowers loosely in the jar, starting with the hydrangeas.

All of the flowers dry nicely. This same combination of flowers could be used for a hand-tied bouquet.

Hand-tied round bouquet

Flowers & Essentials
Blue hydrangeas

Floral supplies

Ribbon

Preparation & Assembly

1. Condition for woody stems (see page 30).

2. Recut under warm water when ready to assemble the bouquet.

3. Assemble in the hand, and bind (see page 34), then finish with a thin satin ribbon and pearl-tipped corsage pins.

Irresistible Iris

Delicate and strikingly beautiful, irises are a bold choice for wedding flowers. They're not only lovely to look at, they're so fragrant that they're often used in perfumes or even in wines to provide "bouquet."

Irises come in an astounding variety of colors, from white with a bright yellow center to pale pink to deep blue-black. There are bi-color, bi-tone, blended, or variegated irises with rich, dramatic color combinations. Their textures vary, too—some are lacy-edged or ruffled, some have sleek-edged petals. There are tall or miniature varieties, and bearded (featuring thick 'hairs' in the center) or beardless types. Check gardening catalogues or online sites for pictures of all the amazing varieties available, and you'll probably find irises hard to resist.

As a cake topper, a single iris surrounded by a few sprigs of trachelium, blue mist, hydrangea, and delphinium is striking against pure white icing.

A series of floating iris heads highlights the beauty of these bowls and makes a modern statement.

flower facts

Botanical Name

Iris

Bloom Time

Mid-spring to early summer

Availability

Late winter through early summer

Hardiness

Fairly fragile; vase life is two to five days

General Care of Irises

Irises should be cut when the buds are starting to emerge from under the leaf sheaves and starting to unfurl very slightly. They will open very quickly once cut. Don't purchase irises that are very tightly closed—they will probably not open—and don't buy flowers that are already in bloom, as they won't last long. Cut irises first thing in the morning if possible, or during a cool time of the day. Cut at a slant and replenish the water often, as they are very thirsty flowers. Add flower food to the water for extended life.

PHOTO BY WWW.GOFORTHPHOTO.COM FLORAL DESIGN PERRI, LTD.

A simple, hand-tied bouquet of Professor Blauuw irises is delicate and understated—perfect for a modern bride, or as a corsage alternative for a mother-of-the bride or other female family member.

interesting iris varieties

*Alizes (white center with
  bright blue-tinted ruffles)*
*Amas (brilliant blue with
  yellow center)*
*Aphrodisiac (pale apricot with
  touches of pink)*
*Above the Clouds (pale blue
  with ruffled petals)*
Dark Passion (deep blue-black)
Ghost Train (midnight blue)
Kentucky Woman (pale pink)
Play with Fire (deep red)

Something Blue

If you're a keen observer of tradition, you'll want to carry something blue on your wedding day. This dreamy bouquet is dotted with stems of electric blue delphinium and tied with a luscious pale blue satin bow. Just a touch of blue is enough to make a bouquet distinctive, and the added height of the delphinium also gives it a sweet, cottage garden feel.

flower facts

Availability
Summer to fall; moderately priced

Hardiness
Delphinium needs to be kept well hydrated, so it's best to keep this bouquet in water as long as possible; the other flowers in the bouquet should be fine for a day out of water

Hand-tied garden-style nosegay

Flowers & Essentials

Electric blue Volkerfrieden delphinium

Vendela roses

Pee gee hydrangea

Fall hydrangea (Nikko blue hydrangea after it turns green)

Sea grass

Sedum

Artemisia

Seeded eucalyptus

Floral supplies

Preparation & Assembly

1. Condition the delphinium for hollow stems (see page 31). The hydrangea and roses can be conditioned for woody stems (see page 30).

2. Gather a small bunch of roses, artemesia, delphinium, and sedum in your hands, spacing out the colors intermittently. Since delphinium is fragile, you'll need to make sure the surrounding flowers support the stems. Add hydrangea, sea grass, and eucalyptus.

3. Bind the bouquet (see page 34), then tie it with a generous amount of wide double-satin ribbon, creating a bow just under the flower heads.

4. Keep the bouquet in water right up until the time of the ceremony or pictures (make sure to blot it dry before handling it). This bouquet will dry well hung upside down in a cool, dark place.

something old, something new

Although you may not remember when or how first heard it, you are sure to be familiar with the wedding superstition that a bride should carry "something old, something new, someting borrowed, something blue" to ensure good luck on her wedding day.

Like most traditions that come down through time, everyone has a theory on what the rhyme means, but no one is exactly sure. According to some accounts, it's an old English tradition with origins dating back into the 16th century. This interpretation says that the "something old" reminds the bride of her family and her life before marriage, the "something new" acknowledges that she is starting a new life, something borrowed represents support from friends, and something blue is a symbol of her fidelity (or purity, depending on who is telling the story). A part of the rhyme which is frequently forgotten is the last line "and a sixpence in her shoe" for prosperity.

No one is really sure how much of all this is accurate, but nonetheless, the tradition continues. A bride often carries something of her mother's for the something old, and a new piece of jewelry to serve as the something new. The something borrowed could be anything from a handkerchief to a hair clip, and blue flowers or ribbons in the bouquet can serve to fulfill the last of the requirements. While you may have trouble finding a sixpence, any lucky coin in your shoe will do.

PHOTO BY WWW.ALLEGRASSTUDIO.COM   FLORAL DESIGN SHERRY SPENCER, PAT'S FLORAL DESIGN

Some Like It Hot

You don't have to be a blushing bride—why not be a radiant one? Flowers in exuberant orange and dynamic yellow are perfect for a summer wedding outdoors or one with a Mediterranean theme. They're a natural choice for fall weddings when the trees are dressed in flaming red, orange, and yellow foliage. Even in the springtime, charming yellow tulips or daffodils are cheerful companions on your wedding day. Consider a bold orange ranunculus bouquet or elegant orange daylilies for the tables. Apricot roses are modern and romantic, and yellow gerbera daisies are delightful. Wedding flowers in orange and yellow will raise the spirits of all who see them.

The Year in Orange & Yellow

SPRING
Crocus
Narcissus (daffodil)
Oriental poppy
Parrot tulip

SUMMER
Coreopsis
Cosmos
Hibiscus
Daylily
Marigold
Nasturtium
Sunflower

FALL
Chinese lantern
Chrysanthemum
Dahlia
*Persimmon and persim-
   mon branch*

WINTER
Acacia
Forsythia
Hellebore
Iceland poppy
Peach poinsettia

YEAR-ROUND
Calla lilies
Rose

Upbeat Orange Roses

This bouquet of roses in harmonious tones of peach and orange perfectly captures the joyful nature of a sunny wedding day. The colors are so uplifting, the texture so appealing, that you can't help but smile when you see it. The design is very basic—simple enough to complement most any type of bridesmaid or bridal gown, and easy for a DIY bride to make.

Hand-tied round bouquet

Flowers & Essentials

Orange macarena spray roses

Orange unique roses

Movie star roses

Floral supplies

Ribbon

Preparation & Assembly

1. Condition according to the instructions for roses (see page 30). When you're ready to assemble the bouquet, recut the stems to the length you want.

2. Gather the flowers in your hand, mixing the varieties of roses somewhat evenly for contrast. Bind the bouquet (see page 34), and wrap the entire bunch with floral tape (up and down the stems). Ordinarily roses need to be wired for support, but in this tight arrangement, the roses support each other. Wrap the bouquet with an ivory ribbon, and secure in place with pearl-tipped corsage pins.

3. Keep the bouquet in water until it will be used, or mist the petals with water when it's out of a vase.

flower facts

Availability
Roses available year-round; moderately priced

Hardiness
Hardy; should last several days with proper conditioning (but should be kept out of direct heat if possible); bruises on light-colored roses show more readily, so try to keep the flower heads protected

Inventive Oranges & Yellows

The bright, sunny hues of orange and yellow
instantly give a welcoming feel to your celebration.

A tiny clutch of bright orange gerbera
daisies surrounded by a collar of
bright green galax leaves provides a
visual pop.

Sunny yellow gerberas are informal and
appealing. The bride tied her "something
old," a vintage handkerchief, around the
stems of the bouquet.

Here's a fresh arrangement idea for a summer wedding (especially one that's held outdoors or seaside). A bowl of oranges of different shapes and sizes garnished with a few marigolds is unique and appealing, not to mention inexpensive and easy to put together. An earthenware bowl gives the arrangement a casual feel, but put the grouping in a cut glass bowl and it can look sleek and contemporary, easily fitting in at a semiformal wedding.

Taking the monochromatic scheme one step further, this appealing table arrangement pairs a bright orange thin-mouthed vase with a few stems of orange ranunculus and orange gerbera daisies. It's an eye-catching combination that really stands out. Both of these flowers bend naturally, which looks great with the curve of the vase.

Seasons

A seasonal approach to wedding flowers is a sensible approach. Regardless of the time of year of your wedding, nature provides a glorious selection of flowers and foliage for you to choose from every season. It's true that these days you can order many flowers out of season, but consider what the season has to offer before writing off seasonal favorites. In spring, tulips just feel right; and in fall, summer colors can seem garish surrounded by the beautiful palette the autumn has to offer. Besides looking lovely in their natural surroundings, seasonal flowers are much more affordable than out-of-season selections—a big plus for the budget-conscious bride. Take a look at the bouquets and arrangements in this section of the book for classic seasonal looks and new interpretations of old favorites.

Spring

The first flowers of spring are a welcome sight after the long months of winter. From fragile lilies of the valley to crisp yellow daffodils and vibrant violets, spring flowers can be unabashedly romantic, refreshingly simple, or quietly elegant—giving you lots of options when it comes to your spring wedding flower plan. You can stick to the traditional with a tiny posy of tender hyacinths, violets, or pansies, or use a nosegay of showy white peonies for a bolder look. If the soft retiring colors of spring aren't quite your speed, go for flame red tulips offset by green foliage or vibrant orange oriental poppies. The beautiful flowering trees and shrubs of spring, such as dogwood, cherry blossom, or apple blossom, are perfect for modern, minimalist arrangements. While you may not be able to count on sunny skies for your spring wedding, you can be sure that finding the perfect flowers will be a breeze.

Spring Flower Highlights

Apple or cherry
  blossom branch
Azalea
Cape jasmine
Forget-me-nots

Hyacinth
Iris
Lady's mantle
  (alchemilla)
Lily of the valley

Mimosa
Narcissus (daffodil,
  narcissus)
Pansy
Peony

Quince branch
Tulip
Viburnum
Violet

Peonies, Plus

Possibly the fairest of all garden flowers, peonies are a natural at weddings. Their sumptuous blooms spill open with layers and layers of tissue-soft petals, and their fragrance is intoxicating. Peonies come in white, red, yellow, peach, and the most popular variety, the pink Sarah Bernhardt peony. These two bouquets demonstrate how versatile peonies can be.

Hand-tied posy

Flowers & Essentials
Pink roses
Yellow roses
Lavender freesia
Pink peonies
Floral supplies

Preparation & Assembly

1. Condition the peonies and roses according to instructions for woody stems (see page 30). The freesia can be conditioned according to the instructions for soft stems (see page 31).

2. Gather a few roses, freesia stems, and peonies in your hand, alternating the flowers for texture and color. Keep adding flowers in a tight bunch until you have a compact mound. Bind and tie the bouquet and wrap with ribbon, leaving bare stems exposed.

3. Keep the bouquet in water for as long as possible to ensure freshness of the peonies.

PHOTO BY WWW.ALLEGRASSTUDIO.COM   FLORAL DESIGN FEARRINGTON HOUSE COUNTRY INN

flower facts

Botanical Name
Paeonia

Bloom Time
Peonies: late April to early June

Availability
Spring only; expensive

Hardiness
Peonies can last for over a week if kept in water; out of water, they will quickly lose their petals; they should be kept in water as long as possible, and care should be taken to avoid touching the flower head and dislodging petals

PHOTO BY WWW.OPPENHEIMPHOTO.COM   FLORAL DESIGN LUCK MCELREATH, THE FLOWER GALLERY

Hand-tied round bouquet

Flowers & Essentials
Sarah Bernhardt peonies
White Miss America peonies
White lilac
Floral supplies
Ribbon

Preparation & Assembly

1. When buying peonies, choose buds that are just opening and are soft to the touch (if they're too hard they probably won't ever open). Condition the peonies and lilac for woody stems (see page 30), and use flower food in the water.

2. Gather the peonies in your hand, then surround the central cluster with lilacs. Bind and tie (see page 34). Wrap the bouquet with a generous amount of double-satin ribbon, then make a bow at the top.

3. Keep the bouquet in the water until the last minute possible, then blot the stems before using.

Tulipamania

Despite its illustrious past as the flower that took Europe by storm in the 17th century, the tulip today has assumed a somewhat humble station in the garden. But don't underestimate its impact in a wedding bouquet or arrangement. It's a remarkably versatile flower that can stand on its own or serve as an accent flower, looking formal and elegant or cheerful and approachable.

flower facts

Botanical Name
Tulipa

Bloom Time
Early spring

Availability
Late winter through early summer; inexpensive

Hardiness
Somewhat fragile, but should last five to eight days

Table arrangement

Flowers & Essentials
Rococo parrot tulips

Immature viburnum

Floral supplies

Preparation & Assembly

1. Tulips should be purchased or cut when their buds are showing color, but not yet open. Condition for soft stems in tepid water. Recut at an angle, taking off white part of bottom of stem (at least 1 inch [2.5 cm]). Remove foliage if desired.

2. Wrap the cut stems in brown paper or even newspaper "sleeves," and bind at the bottom to hold them upright and keep the stems straight while they're hydrating. Place the

stems in a cool place out of the sun-light until ready to use. Keep hydrat-ed. If you want the stems to bend, position them towards light and they will lean toward it.

3. The key to this arrangement (left) is texture and contrast. Pair your "Rococo" parrot tulips with immature viburnum blooms. The red dominates the palette, and the soft green viburnum fills in.

A note on tulips: Don't let tulips share a container with narcissi (paperwhites, daffodils, jonquils, etc.) that have just been cut. Narcissi emit a sap that can shorten a tulip's life. If you do join them in a container, make sure each has been conditioned separately and that the narcissi aren't recut.

a note on tulips

Tulips can become droopy if air gets trapped in their stems. To release the air, prick the stem with a pin just below the flower head. Wrap the stem in waxed tissue, brown paper, or even newspaper, and stand it up in cold water. If you haven't already, add flower food to the water.

tulip varieties

Abba (red, double leaf)

Angelique (white with pink edge leaves)

Casablanca (white, double leaf)

Don Quichotte (deep pink)

Lucky Strike (bright red with white edge)

Peer Gynt (mauve)

Flaming parrot (yellow with red stripes and ruffled edge)

Inzell (snow white)

Monte Carlo (deep yellow, double flower)

Negrita (deep blue-violet)

Rococo (red-orange and green)

Prinses Irene (bright orange)

Attila (purple pink)

Queen of the Night (almost black)

PHOTO BY WWW.UNRUEPHOTO.COM

Slender elegant white tulips set in a tall glass container that supports their stems need no further embellishment. To make the stems spread out in different directions, the stems were allowed to lean in one direction, then separated and spread around the container.

Darling Buds

The first tender blooms to poke their heads above ground in the spring are delicate in shape, proportion, and color. Such precious flowers are best appreciated when there's not a lot to distract attention from their simple beauty. They don't need fancy containers or lots of filler foliage to dress them up. Here are a few ideas for table arrangements that focus on the charm of spring flowers.

flower facts

Botanical Name
Muscari

Bloom Time
Early spring

Availability
In season only; expensive

Hardiness
Should last six days as cut flower

Table arrangement

Flowers & Essentials
Grape hyacinths

Flower pots

Covering: real leaves, silk leaves, or twigs

Hot glue and glue gun

Double-sided adhesive tape (optional)

Preparation & Assembly

To attach the covering to the pot, use double-sided adhesive tape or hot glue (not for some silk leaves, which may melt at high temperatures). Experiment with different materials until you get a look that works with the texture of the flower and mood of your wedding. Some interesting leaves to try are magnolia, silver dollar eucalyptus, banana, or any of the many types of calathea, known for its wide, variegated leaves. You may also consider cinnamon sticks, or pieces of bamboo cut in half to lay flat against the side of the container.

early spring bulb plants

Crocus
Daffodil
Fritillaria
Grape hyacinth
Narcissus
Tulip

Table arrangement

The sweet, fragile flowers of early spring are irresistibly romantic. These tiny blooms look sweet in milkglass eggcups clustered together. Hyacinths plucked from their stems, lily of the valley flowers and leaves, and grape hyacinths sit inside cracked eggs filled with water then placed in the eggcups. Using small, inexpensive (but elegant) containers like this not only makes a unique display, but allows you to send guests home with an arrangement as a wedding keepsake.

Summer

Summer is still the most popular time of the year to get married, and it's easy to see why. Warm summer days and nights seem to guarantee perfect weather, and a memorable event. Your choices for flowers at a summer wedding seem positively endless—it's just a question of narrowing it down. Summer flowers come in every hue, from azure blue and lavender to bright yellow, deep goldenrod, and pure white, so it's a great time for a mixed bouquet highlighting contrasting colors and textures. Roses are the summer wedding classic, but investigate your options before ruling out others. Rhododendrons are gorgeous and unexpected at an early summer wedding. Hydrangeas come in a huge variety of colors, from white or deep purple to old-fashioned pink-tinged or soft blue. Let your imagination run wild for your summer wedding—whatever you're able to dream up, summer is the perfect time to find it.

Sensational Summer Flowers

Allium
Astilbe
Bachelor's buttons
Campanula (bellflower)
Celosia (Cockscomb)
Cosmos

Dahlia
Daisy
Daylily (hemerocallis)
Delphinium
Freesia
Galliardia

Gardenia
Hibiscus
Hydrangea
Lily (Asiatic, etc.)
Nasturtium
Queen Anne's lace

Rose
Scabiosa
  (pincushion flower)
Sunflower
Sweet pea
Veronica

Fresh Greens

The billowy texture and cool green and white color of these hydrangea blossoms are refreshing and inviting for a summer wedding. The bouquet style is elegant but unpretentious, equally at home at a casual or semiformal affair, paired with an antique gown or a modern sheath.

PHOTO WWW.LISAFRECHETTE.COM   FLORAL DESIGN CINDIE ALLEN, THE FLOWER CART AT CLEMENTS' MARKETPLACE

a full, round bouquet. Add budded hydrangea heads as accents to fill out the bouquet, then add salal leaves around the outside to support the inner blooms.

3. Bind the bouquet and finish with 3-inch (7.6 cm) ivory satin dressmaker ribbon and corsage pins.

flower facts

Botanical Name
Hydrangea macrophylla

Availability
Summer through fall. Inexpensive to moderately priced in season; expensive out of season

Hardiness
Will last four to six days as a cut flower if kept well-hydrated

Hand-tied round bouquet

Flowers & Essentials

White and green hydrangea
  macrophylla

Immature hydrangea budded heads

Salal foliage

Floral supplies

Ribbon

Preparation & Assemby

1. Condition the stems according to the procedure for woody stems (see page 30). Let stand in a cool (preferably dark) place overnight.

2. Arrange the blooms (starting with the larger ones) in the hand to make

Woodland Wedding

This sweet bouquet of wildflowers mixed with summer garden blooms creates a magical midsummer feel. Color takes a back-seat to texture in this bouquet—the soft palette and silvery-blue foliage accentuates the composition of delicate flowers. Everything about it is dainty and refined, so it complements a feminine, romantic dress.

Hand-tied posy

Flowers & Essentials

Mariachi cream lisianthus blooms and buds

Versailles freesia

Belladonna light blue delphinium

Cottage yarrow

Queen Anne's lace

Wax flower

Majolika and Ilse spray roses

Pink stock

Pink pepperberries

Seeded eucalyptus

Pittosporum leaves

Galax leaves

Floral supplies

Ribbon

Preparation & Assembly

1. Many of the flowers in this bouquet have leaves and buds that need to be removed. Once the stems have been stripped, condition the flowers according to the instructions for soft stems (see page 31).

2. Assemble the larger blooms in the hand first, then add accent flowers to fill in, and, finally, position the foliage.

3. Bind and wrap as usual (see page 34). Keep in water and out of the heat as long as possible before the wedding, as these blooms are quite fragile.

flower facts

Most of the flowers for this bouquet are garden or wildflowers.

Availability
Summer to early fall

Hardiness
Since many of the stems are fragile, they should be kept well hydrated; they have a short vase life of about 3 days

Bountiful Blue Hydrangeas

This wreath says "celebration" loudly, clearly, and with gusto. A lush, extravagant arrangement like this welcomes guests and sets the tone for an elegant affair. This wouldn't be classified as an inexpensive or easy-to-make wreath, but if you're looking for dramatic impact, it's worth the extra effort and expense.

PHOTO BY WWW.OPPENHEIMPHOTO.COM   FLORAL DESIGN CINDA LAWSON, A FLOWER AFFAIRE

flower facts

Botanical Name
Hydrangea

Bloom Time
Late spring through fall

Availability
Summer and year-round flowers; expensive only because of the amount used

Hardiness
Should last several days if the floral foam is kept wet

Door wreath

Flowers & Essentials

Blue hydrangeas

Pink Anna roses

Porcelana spray roses

Hydrangea leaves

Floral foam wreath holder

Floral supplies

Ribbon

Preparation & Assembly

1. Condition the flowers according to the instructions for woody stems (see page 30), and allow them to soak in a cool place for several hours.

2. Soak a floral foam wreath holder in tepid water (to which flower food has been added) until it sinks.

3. After the flowers have soaked for a few hours, recut the hydrangea stems to about 2 inches (5 cm) below the bloom.

4. Start inserting them into the form. Continue adding blooms until you've covered the form. Wire the roses you'll use (see page 32), and add them in incrementally around the wreath for texture and depth. Add hydrangea foliage as needed for contrast. For this arrangement, the leaves were sprayed with a floral preservative, which seals off the flower, preventing water from evaporating through the petals.

PHOTO BY WWW.ROBERTMARCOS.COM
FLORAL DESIGN ROSITA'S FLOWER SHOP

The same combination of blooms is used on a smaller scale for this tiny flower girl bouquet. Hydrangeas are lightweight, so little hands don't get tired carrying them.

Symphony
in Green & White

Green and white harmonize together perfectly in this lovely bouquet. The overall feel is full and loose, giving the impression of abundance. While green dominates the palette, the tender blooms and touch of white peeking out from opening buds add delicate detail.

PHOTO BY WWW.ELOISEFARR.COM   FLORAL DESIGN JANE DEMPSEY, JANE DEMPSEY STUDIOS

Hand-tied
round bouquet

Flowers & Essentials

White freesia

White snapdragon

Larkspur buds

Lemon leaf

Italian ruscus

White Eskimo roses

Ivy

Rosemary

Floral supplies

Ribbon

Corsage pins

Preparation & Assembly

1. Condition the stems according to their type (see page 30-31). Let them soak overnight in water, then recut at an angle before assembling the bouquet.

2. Assemble the flowers in your hand, adding foliage to fill in.

3. Bind and tie the bouquet with a #10 ribbon, leaving the stems exposed. Finish with pearl-tipped corsage pins.

flower facts

Availability
The flowers in this bouquet are available in spring and summer (some, such as foliage and roses, available year-round)

Hardiness
Not especially delicate

PHOTO BY WWW.ELOISEFARR. COM   FLORAL DESIGN JANE DEMPSEY, JANE DEMPSEY STUDIO

The bride's hair is pulled back into a simple chignon with a piece of white freesia and stat- ice tucked into it.

Fall

Warm, crisp days and cool nights make fall an irresistibly romantic time of year—the perfect time for a wedding dressed with dazzling flowers, fruit, and fall foliage. The rich coppers, ambers, mochas, and mustards of fall offer a versatile palette on which to build your flower plan. From mellow, romantic apricot calla lilies to intense orange ranunculus, there are fall flowers to suit the feel of any wedding. Don't overlook the bounty of the fall harvest: gorgeous ripe apples and pumpkins and gourds make enchanting additions to table displays. Dried plants, such as Chinese lanterns, bittersweet vine, or even wheat sheaves are seasonal delights. If your wedding is held in an area with brilliant fall foliage, you can incorporate it into your table arrangements to great effect. If you have your heart set on cream roses, you're in luck. You can order roses (and many other flowers) in any season, so chances are they'll be available too. But before you dismiss fall flowers altogether, take a look at the following section for ideas that take fall flowers to a new level of elegance.

Fantastic Fall Flowers

Aster	Coneflower	Heather
Bittersweet vine	Dahlia	Marigold
Chinese lantern (physalis alkekengi)	Daylily	Stonecrop (sedum "Autumn Joy")
Chrysanthemum	Globe amaranth	Zinnia
	Globe thistle	

Autumn Elegance

This sophisticated fall bouquet starts with mango calla lilies surrounded by loose blades of bear grass. Wheat sheaths, perhaps the original bridal bouquet, have been carried down the aisle since ancient times. In the past, they symbolized fertility and prosperity for the new couple. Today, they're just a reminder that fall is harvest time, and they add a nice bit of texture to a fall bouquet.

flower facts

Availability
All the materials are available year-round.

Hardiness
Calla lilies need to be well hydrated; they should last three to five days as a cut flower

Hand-tied presentation bouquet

Flowers & Essentials
Mango calla lilies
Bear grass
Wheat sheaths
Floral supplies
Raffia

Preparation & Assembly

1. Condition the calla lilies according to the instructions for hollow stems (see page 31). Let them drink in water in a cool dark place overnight.

2. When you're ready to make the bouquet, place a few wheat sheaths and blades of bear grass on the table. Add the calla lilies on top one by one in an arrow shape, staggering the height. Before you bind the bouquet, add a few galax leaves at the base of the lowest flower heads.

3. Bind the arrangement (see page 34), then cut the stems to the desired length. Tie over the binding with raffia.

PHOTOS BY WWW.OPPENHEIMPHOTO.COM   FLORAL DESIGN LEIGH LUNSFORD, RIDDLE'S FLOWER SHOP

Fall in Love

Celebrating the spirit of the season, each of these arrangements captures the essence of fall at its finest—the color, the textures, and the warmth (despite the chill in the air). Fall weddings have a special kind of magic, especially if they're held outdoors. Using seasonal flowers and foliage brings the lighthearted mood of fall into the wedding celebration.

Taking full advantage of beautiful local fall foliage, this earthy arrangement (seated in a copper bowl) features bittersweet vine, red spray roses, and sphagnum moss. The short, round nature of the bowl suits the arrangement perfectly—the flowers and foliage stay close to the lip of the bowl and spill over, giving the impression of abundance.

PHOTO BY WWW.ELOISEFARR.COM FLORAL DESIGN EVE DAVIS, WWW.HAWKANDIVY.COM

A cheerful pot of mums looks charming sprouting from a pumpkin on the bride and groom's table. But you can still get this look even if you can't see yourself carving pumpkins on your wedding day. This pleasantly plump one is actually an impostor—a hollow foam pumpkin from a craft store. The mums, still in their pot, are simply placed inside it. A layer of moss (also from a craft store) fills out the top of the mum pot and spills over, and a wreath of dried grapevine circles the pumpkin's base. Small gourds, leaves, and acorns are placed around the arrangement to complete the look.

PHOTO BY WWW.ELOISEFARR.COM   FLORAL DESIGN AMY KOTTWITZ

This nostalgic cake perfectly captures the feel of a fall wedding. Nasturtium, pansies, and lavender skirt the cake, adding color. As an added bonus, they're all edible.

PHOTOS BY WWW.OPPENHEIMPHOTO.COM   CAKE DESIGN DONNA LANCE

Autumn Orchids

At a time of year when flowers and foliage tend more toward the sensible and earthy, a bouquet of orchids is a flight of fancy. It seems almost impossible that such an exotic tropical flower comes in such rich fall colors, but luckily for brides, it does. Paired with a collar of eucalyptus pods, this is a striking, distinctive fall bouquet.

flower facts

Availability
Available year-round; relatively expensive

Hardiness
Orchids can last up to a week in properly conditioned; eucalyptus pods can be used dried

Hand-tied round bouquet

Flowers & Essentials
Large eucalyptus pods
Chocolate cymbidium orchids
22-gauge wire
Floral supplies
Organza ribbon

Preparation & Assembly

1. Condition the orchids by leaving them on the stem (with the stem submerged), and misting them lightly with water.

2. Cut the orchids from their stems, leaving about a ¼-inch (6 mm) stem. Wire the orchids with 22-gauge wire and wrap with floral tape (see page 32).

3. Take a cluster of the orchids in your hand, then begin surrounding them with the eucalyptus pods until you have a full round bouquet. Bind the bouquet (see page 34). Tie it with organza ribbon.

Winter

If your plans call for a winter wedding, don't despair on the flower front. While your choices may not be as abundant as those available to a summer bride, a winter wedding offers unexpected opportunities for creative bouquets and arrangements. Winter wedding flowers are all about drama—think bright red berries against pure white snow and tall-stemmed amaryllis that seem downright tropical. Flowers in deep saturated colors, like claret and eggplant, paired with textured foliage are a striking combination for bouquets or arrangements, and velvet ribbons in black, lapis, or gold add the perfect finishing touch. Tiny beaded inserts may be too much in a summer bouquet, but in the winter they sparkle in the candlelight and cast out winter gloom.

Don't forget, too, that you can order many off-season flowers during the winter, and there are a variety of flowers that are available year-round. If your wedding is held in a church, hotel, or other public space, you may need only to make bouquets and table arrangements, since holiday trees, wreaths, and garlands will be there for you to enjoy. Take a look at the following section for ideas on how to breathe new life into classic winter flowers and create unexpected combinations in bouquets and arrangements.

Winter Flowers

Acacia
Amaryllis
Camellia
Cyclamen
Forsythia
Hellebore (Lenten rose)
Iceland poppy

Juniper
Mistletoe
Narcissus (paperwhite)
Poppy anemone
Poinsettia
Snowberry
  (symphoricarpos)

Snowdrop
Stephanotis
Winterberry holly
  (ilex verticillata)
Winter heath
Winter jasmine

Wintery Mix

Interesting textures and saturated color make this an intriguing and sophisticated bouquet for a winter wedding. Contrasted against rich, dark velvets or even wintery whites, it's just a little bit decadent.

flower facts

Availability

Roses and calla lilies can be ordered year-round; lace-leaf hydrangea is a late summer-fall bloom that can be ordered into the late fall/early winter; viburnum berries, berzillia berries, and maple leaves can be ordered fall through winter

Hardiness

This bouquet should be kept well hydrated; the foliage is hardy, but the callas will last only a few days

Hand-tied round bouquet

Flowers & Essentials

Eggplant calla lilies

White Vendela roses

Lace-leaf hydrangeas

Frosted berzillia berries

Green viburnum berries

Maple leaves

Floral supplies

Ribbon

Preparation & Assembly

1. Condition the calla lilies according to the instructions for hollow stems, and the roses according to their special conditioning (see page 30). Remove excess leaves from the maple foliage, and remove the viburnum berries from their branches.

2. Assemble the calla lilies, roses, and hydrangeas in your hand. Add a few viburnum berries between the flowers. Surround the flowers with berzillia berries, then add a few stems of maple leaves.

3. Bind and wrap the bouquet with velvet ribbon.

FLORAL DESIGN WWW.BLOOM-ROOM.COM

Berry Beautiful

In winter, when flowers seem in short supply, berries are at their peak. From the vibrant red of winterberries to the charming white and pink of snowberries and the yellow, blue, or purple of viburnum berries, there are several options for adding winter color and texture to an arrangement or bouquet.

A tall, frosted vase shows off the simple beauty of long branches of winterberry. Look for branches that are still very full, and handle carefully, as the berries can easily dislodge and the branch become bare. Condition for woody stems (see page 30).

PHOTO BY WWW.PARKERCSMITH.COM   FLORAL DESIGN: GREGORY BROWN (AIFD), FOXGLOVES AND IVY FLORAL DESIGN STUDIO

When ordering winterberries, order more than you think you'll need. The berries are fragile and can detach from the branches easily when moved.

berry basics

Common Names
Common winterberry, Snowberry

Botanical Names
Ilex verticillata, Symphoricarpos albus, opulus, nudum

Bloom Time
Winterberries appear in early winter, usually November and December; Snowberries appear in late summer through early winter

Availability
Winterberry: November through January; expense relative to length of branch, ranging from moderate to expensive

Snowberry: Summer through December

Hardiness
Very hardy (can last up to two weeks)

Snowberries have relatively thin stems, so they do better in short vases that can support their weight. A few holly leaves are mixed in with this arrangement for texture.

flower facts

Botanical Name
Amaryllis belladonna,
Hippeastrum amaryllis (hybrid)

Other Names
Magic lily, resurrection lily

Bloom time
Early cultivars bloom in
December, late-flowering types
in January and February

Availability
December through February

Hardiness
Can last up to three weeks with
proper conditioning and care

Arty Amaryllis Bouquet

Bold, splashy amaryllis is a breath of fresh air during the chilly, gray months of winter. Its tall, dramatic stalk has a modern, architectural feel, and its oversized flowers emit an intense fragrance. This bouquet features unopened buds, giving it a distinctive, hothouse flower feel. Amaryllis stems come with two to five blooms per stem, and dozens of colors from white, pink, and red to two-tone and variegated styles. There are miniature varieties, too, which look more like orchids. A single stem of amaryllis or a series of single stems also makes a great table arrangement. Use tall, glass vases that show off the flower's graceful stem.

Hand-tied presentation bouquet

Flowers & Essentials
Amaryllis stems
Ribbon
Floral supplies

Preparation & Assembly

1. Purchase amaryllis when the buds are showing color but not yet open. Condition the flowers according to the instructions for hollow stems (see page 31). Amaryllis desperately need water, so let them soak in tepid water with flower food for as long as possible.

2. When you're ready, tie the stems below the flowerheads, then trim the stems as necessary.

Poinsettia Rediscovered

Poinsettias have a bit of an image problem. Come December they're ubiquitous, showing up everywhere from grocery stores to office lobbies, sitting in plastic pots wrapped in red foil.

But if you can look beyond the packaging, poinsettias are gorgeous tropical flowers, available in over 100 varieties, with colors ranging from the familiar bright red to pink, white, green, or salmon. The tinge of color on the leaves is spectacular, with just a trace of color around the veins and edges. Throw out the plastic pots and give poinsettias a makeover in a simple modern flowerpot. This display is dramatic because of the uniformity of the containers and the shapes of the poinsettias.

flower facts

Botanical Name
Euphorbia pulcherrima

Other Names
Christmas plant, lobster flower, flame plant

Availability
Available late November through February

Hardiness
Should last several weeks potted; as a cut flower it can last five days.

Note: A fresh poinsettia is one on which little or no yellow pollen is showing on the flower clusters in the center of the "bracts" (the part that looks like a flower). Keep the plant in a warm spot indoors. If you use poinsettias as a cut flower, condition them for milky stems (see page 31).

Wild at Heart

Wildflowers are a refreshing change from traditional wedding flowers. They're a natural choice for a not-so-formal wedding or one held outdoors, but they also lend a homey feeling to an otherwise ordinary church or hotel wedding. Wildflowers are an attractive option for the DIY bride because they're easy to grow at home with reliable results. They're not easy to find out of season, though. If you do order them from a florist or local grower, you'll need to choose from what nature has to offer at the time of your wedding. If casual, relaxed, and unpretentious describes your wedding style, consider the bouquets and arrangements in this section.

Stylish Sunflowers

flower facts

Botanical Name
Helianthus

Availability
Summer into the fall; inexpensive

Hardiness
If given plenty of water and a little flower food, can last up to two weeks as a cut flower

Sunflowers have evolved from their humble position in the field to become a sought-after flower for bouquets and arrangements. A few sunflowers punctuating a bouquet of delicate wildflowers is lovely, but a single stem of a giant sunflower is often enough for a dramatic table setting or aisle decoration. Sunflowers come in lots of sizes (from mini to giant) and colors (from lemon yellow to gold, pink to red, cream to brown), so you're bound to find a variety that suits your needs. They're a reliable flower to choose if you're thinking of growing your own flowers for your wedding day—they're almost guaranteed to come up at the same time every year.

Cascade bouquet

Flowers & Essentials

Sunflowers

Button mums

Dahlia

Seeded eucalyptus

Lemon leaves

Wheat sheaves

Floral supplies

22 to 24 gauge floral wire

Floral tape

Raffia

Bouquet holder

Preparation & Assembly

1. Since this is a wired bouquet, cut all the flowers from their stems and wire them (see page 32).

2. Gather the sunflowers, button mums, and dahlia in your hand, then surround them with seeded eucalyptus, wheat sheaves, and finally lemon leaves.

3. Wrap floral tape around all the wire stems and insert them into the bouquet holder. Tie a long strand of raffia at the top of the bouquet holder.

Cake topper

The single non-pollinating California sunflower on the top layer of this wedding cake sits on a bed of ivy with a few sprays of hypericum berries added for a late summer seasonal touch. On the next layer down, a few hybrid delphinium blossoms join scattered ivy leaves. All the flowers and foliage are hardy enough to withstand a day on the cake without wilting.

PHOTO BY WWW.ELOISEFARR.COM
FLORAL DESIGN PAM HEDSTROM, FLOWER MARKET

distinctive sunflower varieties

Jade (green petals with green center)
Sunbeam (bright yellow with green center)
Sunspot (giant yellow)
Primrose (classic yellow)
Prado red (dark burgundy)
Ruby eclipse (black center with yellow-tipped red petals)
Sundance kid (bronze or yellow, double flower)
Taiyo (has a very large eye)
Teddy bear (yellow, looks like a chrysanthemum)

PHOTO BY WWW.OPPENHEIMPHOTO.COM   FLORAL DESIGN KIRSTEN RIFENBERG-WELLMAN

PHOTO BY WWW.ELOISEFARR.COM   FLORAL DESIGN STEPHEN
BROWN, ASHEVILLE WEDDING FLORIST

Pet garland

These faithful companions are resplendent in their sunflower garlands, made from sunflowers left over from rehearsal dinner table arrangements and aster and goldenrod picked from the field where the wedding took place. The bride and bridesmaids gathered handfuls of flowers and wired them to twine (see garland instructions, page 40). The trick was to cut the twine to a comfortable length for the dog—not too tight, but not loose enough for the dog to step through (hold the twine up to the dog's neck to measure). This was an easy and pleasant project to complete on a late summer wedding day.

Boutonniere

A single miniature sunflower is a striking boutonniere for a summer or early fall wedding. Since the flower head is heavy, it's best to wire a sunflower for a boutonniere (see page 32), rather then simply wrapping the stem and/or adding foliage.

In Love with Lavender

Centuries before flowers made their debut at weddings, brides were carrying herbs down the aisle. In ancient Greece, mint and marigold were the bouquets of choice, doubling as aphrodisiacs to entice the groom. Through the years, flowers came into fashion, but herbs are still an appealing choice for a bouquet.

Lavender, one of the most beautiful and fragrant herbs, is a heavenly alternative to flowers. Its fragrance is legendary, and its flowers come in a spectrum of purples, and even pink and white, too. With a bouquet of lavender (or other flowering herb), you won't have to worry about wilting, and you may even be able to pluck it from your own garden. It dries well, so you'll be able to enjoy the fragrance of your bouquet for years to come.

Lavender bouquet

Flowers & Essentials

Lavender

Floral Supplies

Ribon

Preparation & Assembly

1. If you are using lavender from your garden, cut it just before the last flowers on the flower spikes have opened.

2. Bind and tie it into a bouquet (see page 34), or use it in an arrangement with other herbs or flowers.

To dry lavender, hang it upside down in a warm, airy place (remove the leaves if desired).

flower facts

Botanical Name
Lavendula

Bloom Time
April through September (dependent on variety)

Availability
Easy to find in season, moderately priced; can be found dried out of season

Hardiness
Stems of fresh lavender are flimsy, so they should be tied tightly for support

herbs for foliage

Herbs in place of foliage fill out a bouquet or arrangement beautifully and smell divine. Consider using these herbs as filler, or for color and texture:

Bay

Comfrey

Eucalyptus

Mint

Rosemary

Sage

St. John's Wort
  (hypericum berries)

Thistle

Thyme

Yarrow

A tiny bunch of herbs tied with a thin ribbon is a gracious touch at a guest's table setting. It also serves as a fragrant wedding keepsake for guests to take home.

Daisy Crazy

Think back to your first ideas of romance, and you'll probably think of the daisy. Playing "he loves me, he loves me not," with petals from the daisies in your mom's garden probably kept you entertained for hours and started you dreaming of your wedding day. Now that it's finally here, remember your old friend the daisy. It's a sweet, charming flower, and more versatile than you might think.

flower facts

Botanical Names
Anthemis, Argyranthemum, Bellis, Leucanthemum

Other Names
Marguerite, Shasta daisy, English daisy,

Bloom Time
Late spring to fall

Availability
Inexpensive, available in season

Hardiness
Will last around five days as a cut flower if kept well hydrated

Daisies, ivy, and statice are a casual, charming combination for a pew end arrangement in an attractive bucket. Strands of ivy are wired and looped through the top of the bucket to create a handle.

PHOTO BY WWW.GOFORTHPHOTO.COM FLORAL DESIGN PERRI, LTD.

Flower girls in daisy halos are adorable. The daisies stems are cut to about 2 inches (5.2 cm), then wired (see page 32) and attached to a halo (see page 41 for instructions). Although daisies are a casual flower, they don't look out of place at a semi-formal wedding.

PHOTO BY WWW.GOFORTHPHOTO.COM

PHOTO BY WWW.ELOISEFARR.COM   CAKE DESIGN DARCI DEWULF CAKES

At an outdoor garden wedding on a glorious summer day, daisies and their fellow field and garden flowers are a sweet touch for a simple cake. This design features gerbera daisies, shasta daisies, alstromeria, and clary sage flowers. The flowers sit atop a bed of silvery artemesia "Powis Castle."

Flowers of the Field

For a casual country wedding, wildflowers are the perfect complement. They look informal, but add a homey quality to a celebration. Better still, you can find bountiful wildflowers everywhere in summer—you can pick them right out of your backyard, or even from the side of the road! Just because they're easy to find doesn't mean they're not special. Take a second look at some common wildflowers. Out of their familiar context, you can better appreciate their beauty.

Table arrangement

Flowers & Essentials

Queen Anne's lace

Floral Supplies

Preparation & Assembly

1. If you're cutting from your garden (which you most likely will be since this isn't considered a "florist flower"), cut in the cool of the morning and plunge immediately into water.

2. Remove extra foliage. When using this flower as the only type of flower in an arrangement, be generous with your number of stems. This arrangement looks great because of its fullness. The wide mouth and slender stem of the vase balance out the full "head" of the flowers. Keep well hydrated and the arrangement should last up to a week. The flowers can also be dried in the vase or hanging upside down. Take care not to touch the flower head, which becomes very fragile when dry.

flower facts

Botanical Name
Anthriscus sylvestris

Other Names
Queen Anne's lace, Cow parsley, Wild Carrot

Bloom Time
Summer to fall

Availability
In season (summer to fall); inexpensive

Hardiness
Hardy, but avoid direct sunlight for prolonged periods

PHOTO BY WWW.ELOISEFARR.COM FLORAL DESIGN DENISE SHELTON, SUNSHINE FLORIST

Door arrangement

Flowers & Essentials

Asparagus fern

Delphinium

Flat fern

Iris

Lisanthus

Pink daises

Spider mums

Wax weed

White larkspur

Floral supplies

Waterproof plastic lining

Floral foam

Preparation & Assembly

1. This arrangement should be made the day of the wedding. Start by lining your container with plastic to prevent water leaks, then add a piece of wet floral foam in the bottom of the container.

2. Position your mums in the floral foam as "anchor" flowers. You'll need to keep most of the stems short so that the flowers will be compact and close to the edge of the container, but some of them can keep taller stems to add height to the arrangement.

3. Begin adding your filler flowers to fill out the arrangement. Add delphinium with tall stems in the center for height. The cone shape of the container echoes the shape of the arrangement—a point at the top that spreads out to a triangle at the base. Let the aspargus fern trail over the edge of the container and out the sides. Continue adding flowers till you have a look that's full in the front and on the sides (it can be flat in the back, since it will be attached to a door).

Inspired Ideas

Still haven't found what you're looking for? Maybe you just need a little inspiration. In the following section, you'll find great ideas to use as part of a bigger flower plan, or in place of one. Any of the ideas can be used year-round, at weddings large or small. They're simple, beautiful solutions for a bride on a budget who wants to have memorable flowers without breaking the bank.

PHOTOS, LEFT TO RIGHT: WWW.UNRUEPHOTO.COM, WWW.OPPENHEIMPHOTO.COM, WWW.ELOISEFARR.COM

Thank you for sharing our day.
Love, Ronnie & Lisa

Petal Power

Flower petals conjure up a sense of romance. Scattering petals at your ceremony and reception is just another way to create mood and atmosphere, making it feel a little more magical. If you plan to use a lot of petals, ask your florist or whoever supplies your flowers if you might be able to get a few bags of petals for free. This is a good question to ask in advance so that the florist will have a few days to collect petals for you. The other way to go, of course, is to pick the petals from the flowers yourself (or have friends and helpers do it for you). Check out these inspiring ideas for using petals at your wedding.

You may have seen an aisle of petals before, but this one is distinctive. The trick is to use petals in different colors, and pile them on thickly (a thinly-petaled aisle looks uninspiring).

PHOTO BY WWW.OPPENHEIMPHOTO.COM

A basket of pink "Anna"" rose petals plucked from their stems is an ideal solution for a young flower girl. While carrying a bouquet or kissing ball may work well for older girls, they may be too heavy or require too much concentration for a little one. Throwing petals down the aisle is a great way to give a "big girl" job to a little one, making her feel included in the ceremony. It's also a great distraction to help her get over the jitters caused by walking down the aisle.

Flower petals don't have to be reserved for the ceremony. Scatter them around your guest tables (and even on the floor, if you won't be using it for dancing) at the reception—you'll be surprised how festive the effect will be.

Happily Single

Weddings are all about togetherness and unity. But truth be told, flowers can do just fine on their own, thank you. Without all the distractions of foliage and such, it's easy to appreciate the beauty of a single flower. An arrangement or bouquet featuring a single flower is simplicity itself. It inspires contemplation instead of awe, and proves that less really is more.

If you're a little nervous about sending a single flower out into your wedding all alone, try a cluster or series of singles each in its own container for impact. If you've got an interesting collection of containers, this is a great way to focus attention on the container instead of the flower.

Whether you choose a fragile bud or a flower with a strong stalk and a striking flower head, a single flower can be a great choice for a bouquet or table arrangement, and as an added incentive, you may save on your flower budget, too.

Thank you for sharing our day.
Love, Ronnie & Lisa

Tiny, inexpensive bud vases look perfectly full and balanced when holding a single, substantial flower like this gerbera daisy. There's a hidden advantage to a single-flower arrangement like this: you can give one to each of your guests to take home as a keepsake.

A single flower (in this case, a cream-colored mini gerbera daisy) as a cake topper looks modern and sophisticated. Since lots of weddings now feature individual cakes or cupcakes instead of a cake, this is a great solution for making each individual dessert special.

PHOTO BY WWW.ELOISEFARR.COM   CAKE DESIGN: MARCI MOERMAN

A single magnolia is magnificent in place of a bouquet.

INDEX

CONTRIBUTING FLORAL DESIGNERS

Cindie Allen, The Flower Cart at
  Clement's Marketplace
Portsmouth, Rhode Island

Tam Ashworth, Isari at Four Seasons Aviara
Carlsbad, California

Felicity Banford Floral Design
Millbrook, New York

Gregory Brown, AIFD, Foxgloves and Ivy
Atlanta, Georgia

Stacey Brown, The Bloom Room
Asheville, North Carolina

Stephen Brown, Asheville Wedding Florist
Skyland, North Carolina

Carla Bruce, Petals and Plants
Lynchburg, Virginia

Jill Chaffin Floral Design
Seacliff, New York

Cleary Creations
San Diego, California

The Coordinator, Inc.
Orlando, Florida

Eve Davis, Hawk and Ivy Country Bed and
  Breakfast Retreat
Barnardsville, North Carolina

Pamela DeArras, Coleman Bros.
  Flowers, Inc.
Richmond, Virginia

Jane Dempsey, Jane Dempsey Studios
Spartanburg, South Carolina

Darci DeWulf Cakes
Marshall, North Carolina

Paul Eckhart, Broadway Florists
Newport, Rhode Island

Events by Krawcheck
Charleston, South Carolina

Golden Cricket
Asheville, North Carolina

The Fearrington House Country Inn
  and Restaurant
Pittsboro, North Carolina

Carolyn Gregg, Carolyn Gregg Flowers
New York, New York

Ann Guill, Debra Gladstone, and
  Annette Deleot
Winston-Salem, North Carolina

Pam Hedstrom, Flower Market
Hendersonville, North Carolina

Stacey Howerton
Hot Springs, North Carolina

Jolli Howlett, Botanica Flowers
North Kingstown, Rhode Island

Alex Imidi and Jeff Johnson, Square Root
Santa Ana, California

Amy Kottwitz
Fletcher, North Carolina

Julie Lapham Designs
Southborough, Massachussetts

Cinda Lawson, A Flower Affaire
Suwanee, Georgia

Ann Martin, European Floral
Tampa, Florida

Luck McElreath, The Flower Gallery
Asheville, North Carolina

Marcy Moerman
Asheville, Noth Carolina

Perri, Ltd.
Asheville, North Carolina

Amanda Pickering, Ivie's
Salmouth, Massachusetts

Kristi Podsiadlo, Dahlia, A Florist
Greenville, South Carolina

Kirsten Riffenburg-Wellman
Asheville, North Carolina

Rosita's Flower Shop
San Diego, California

Denise Shelton, Sunshine Florist
Marshall, North Carolina

Sherry Spencer, Pat's Floral Designs
Madison, Virginia

Carly Rose Streiff, Botanical Images
Costa Mesa, California

Nisie Vorachard, Enchanted Florist
Los Alamitos, California

Walt Disney World Florist at
  Walt Disney World
Lake Buena Vista, Florida